How to become a
Help Desk Analyst

James Relington

DEDICATION

This book is dedicated to all the professionals working tirelessly to secure digital systems and protect organizations from ever-evolving threats. To the cybersecurity teams, IT administrators, and identity management experts who ensure safe and seamless access for users—your work is invaluable. And to my family and friends, whose support and encouragement made this journey possible, thank you.

AKNOWLEDGEMENTS

I would like to express my deepest gratitude to everyone who contributed to the creation of this book. To my colleagues and mentors in the cybersecurity field, your insights and expertise have been invaluable. To the organizations and professionals who shared their experiences and best practices, your contributions have enriched this work. A special thank you to my family and friends for their unwavering support and encouragement throughout this journey. Finally, to the readers, thank you for your interest in identity lifecycle management—may this book help you navigate the evolving landscape of digital security with confidence.

Introduction to the Helpdesk Role

The role of a helpdesk analyst, also known as a service desk analyst, is one of the most essential positions in the IT industry. Helpdesk professionals are the first point of contact for users experiencing technical issues, and their ability to diagnose, troubleshoot, and resolve problems efficiently is crucial for maintaining business operations. Organizations rely on their helpdesk teams to ensure that employees, customers, and clients can access the technology they need without disruption. This job requires a combination of technical expertise, communication skills, patience, and problem-solving abilities, making it a dynamic and rewarding career path for those interested in IT support.

A helpdesk analyst's primary responsibility is to provide technical assistance to users experiencing issues with hardware, software, networks, or applications. These problems can range from simple password resets to complex system failures that require in-depth troubleshooting. Helpdesk analysts typically handle these issues through various channels, including phone calls, emails, live chat, and ticketing systems. Their ability to assess the urgency of a problem, prioritize tasks, and provide timely resolutions ensures that business operations continue without significant disruptions. Additionally, they serve as a bridge between end users and IT departments, translating technical jargon into understandable solutions for non-technical individuals.

The demand for helpdesk analysts has grown significantly due to the increasing reliance on technology in almost every industry. Companies of all sizes, from small businesses to multinational corporations, require IT support to manage their infrastructure, maintain cybersecurity, and provide efficient solutions to technical challenges. Many professionals begin their careers in IT as helpdesk analysts before advancing to more specialized roles such as system administration, network engineering, cybersecurity, or IT management. The experience gained in a helpdesk position is invaluable, as it provides a strong foundation in troubleshooting, communication, and customer service—skills that are transferable across multiple IT domains.

One of the most important qualities of a successful helpdesk analyst is strong problem-solving ability. Each day presents a new set of challenges, and analysts must quickly identify the root cause of technical issues and apply logical troubleshooting steps to resolve them. This process often involves asking users detailed questions, replicating errors, researching potential solutions, and utilizing available resources such as knowledge bases, documentation, or senior IT staff. The ability to think critically and remain calm under pressure is essential, especially when dealing with frustrated or non-technical users who rely on the helpdesk for immediate assistance.

Excellent communication skills are another key requirement for helpdesk analysts. Since they interact with users from different backgrounds, industries, and technical skill levels, they must be able to explain technical concepts in a way that is easy to understand. The ability to listen actively, ask the right questions, and provide clear, concise instructions is critical for ensuring that users feel supported and confident in the resolution process. Moreover, a professional and empathetic approach can make a significant difference in user satisfaction, as many individuals who reach out to the helpdesk may be stressed or frustrated due to their technical issues.

Technical knowledge is, of course, a fundamental component of the helpdesk role. Analysts must have a strong understanding of operating systems, networking, hardware, software applications, and common troubleshooting techniques. Many helpdesk positions require familiarity with Windows, macOS, and Linux, as well as experience with enterprise tools such as Microsoft 365, Google Workspace, and remote desktop applications. Additionally, knowledge of ITIL (Information Technology Infrastructure Library) best practices, Active Directory, cybersecurity fundamentals, and ticketing systems can be advantageous for those looking to advance in their careers. While formal education in IT can be beneficial, many helpdesk analysts develop their skills through certifications, self-study, and hands-on experience.

A helpdesk analyst's work environment can vary depending on the organization. Some work in dedicated IT support centers, providing assistance to internal employees, while others may work for managed service providers (MSPs) that offer technical support to multiple clients. With the rise of remote work and cloud-based technologies, many helpdesk analysts now operate in virtual environments, using remote access tools to diagnose and resolve issues without being physically present. Regardless of the setting, adaptability and a willingness to continuously learn are crucial, as technology evolves rapidly and new challenges emerge regularly.

Another important aspect of the helpdesk role is documentation. Maintaining accurate records of incidents, solutions, and recurring problems helps improve efficiency and ensures that knowledge is shared among team members. Many organizations utilize ticketing systems to track and manage user requests, allowing analysts to review past cases and apply previous solutions to similar issues. Proper documentation also plays a role in long-term improvements, as analyzing trends in reported problems can help IT teams develop preventative measures and optimize system performance.

Working in a helpdesk role can be both challenging and rewarding. While it requires patience and resilience, especially when dealing with repetitive issues or difficult users, it also provides a sense of accomplishment when successfully resolving problems and helping others. Many analysts find great satisfaction in troubleshooting complex issues, learning new technologies, and building relationships with users and colleagues. The helpdesk environment fosters continuous learning, as analysts are exposed to a wide range of technical challenges that prepare them for more advanced IT roles in the future.

For those considering a career as a helpdesk analyst, there are several pathways to getting started. Some individuals enter the field with formal IT degrees, while others gain relevant experience through certifications such as CompTIA A+, Microsoft Certified: Modern Desktop Administrator Associate, or ITIL Foundation. Hands-on experience, whether through internships, volunteer work, or personal projects, can also be beneficial in developing the skills necessary for the role. Employers often look for candidates with a strong technical foundation, excellent communication abilities, and a customer-centric mindset.

Ultimately, the helpdesk analyst role is a gateway to the IT industry, offering professionals the opportunity to develop a wide range of skills that can lead to numerous career advancement opportunities. Whether working in a corporate IT department, a managed service provider, or a remote support team, helpdesk analysts play a vital role in ensuring the smooth operation of technology systems across various industries. Those who excel in this field will find that the experience gained at the helpdesk can open doors to more specialized and higher-level positions, making it an excellent starting point for anyone interested in a career in information technology.

Understanding IT Support and Service Desk Operations

IT support and service desk operations are critical components of any organization that relies on technology for daily functions. Businesses, government agencies, educational institutions, and healthcare providers all depend on IT services to ensure that systems remain operational, employees can perform their duties, and customers receive uninterrupted service. The service desk serves as the first line of support, handling technical issues, resolving incidents, and ensuring that users have access to the resources they need. Without a well-functioning IT support system, even minor technical problems can escalate, leading to downtime, decreased productivity, and financial losses. Understanding the structure, processes, and best practices of IT support and service desk operations is essential for anyone considering a career in this field.

IT support can be categorized into different levels, often referred to as tiers. Tier 1 support, also known as the frontline helpdesk, is responsible for handling basic user issues such as password resets, software installations, and general troubleshooting. Tier 2 support involves more advanced troubleshooting and may require access to system configurations, network diagnostics, and in-depth application support. Tier 3 support consists of specialized experts who deal with complex technical problems, system bugs, and infrastructure-related issues. In some cases, organizations have a Tier 4 support level, which includes external vendors and software providers who assist with proprietary systems. Understanding these support levels helps IT professionals determine when to escalate an issue and ensures that problems are handled by the appropriate personnel.

The service desk operates based on structured workflows and best practices to manage incidents efficiently. One of the most widely used frameworks for IT service management is the Information Technology Infrastructure Library (ITIL). ITIL provides guidelines on how to handle incidents, service requests, problem management, and change control. When a user reports an issue, the service desk logs it as an incident in a ticketing system, categorizes it based on severity, and assigns it to the appropriate support personnel. Service Level Agreements (SLAs) define the expected response and resolution times, ensuring that IT teams address problems promptly and consistently. Properly following these procedures helps organizations minimize disruptions and maintain operational efficiency.

A well-structured IT support system relies on ticketing software to track and manage issues. These ticketing systems, such as ServiceNow, Jira Service Management, Freshservice, and Zendesk, allow IT teams to document user requests, update progress, and maintain a historical record of incidents. Tickets contain essential details, including the reported problem, troubleshooting steps taken, and resolution notes. This documentation is invaluable for future reference, helping support teams recognize recurring issues and implement proactive measures to prevent future disruptions. Additionally, well-maintained records provide insights that can be used for process improvement and strategic IT planning.

Communication is a fundamental aspect of service desk operations. IT support professionals must effectively communicate with users who may have varying levels of technical knowledge. The ability to explain solutions in simple terms, ask relevant questions, and provide clear instructions ensures a smooth resolution process. In many cases, users may be frustrated or anxious about their technical issues, making empathy and patience essential skills for service desk analysts. Providing excellent customer service not only resolves technical problems but also builds trust between IT departments and the users they support. A positive support experience can improve user satisfaction and encourage employees to seek IT assistance when needed, rather than attempting to fix issues themselves and potentially causing further complications.

Remote support has become a standard component of IT service desk operations. With businesses shifting toward remote and hybrid work environments, IT teams must be equipped with tools that allow them to assist users regardless of their physical location. Remote desktop software, such as TeamViewer, AnyDesk, and Microsoft Remote Desktop, enables IT professionals to access user devices, diagnose problems, and implement solutions without requiring in-person intervention. Cloud-based IT support platforms also allow service desk teams to manage tickets, monitor systems, and deploy updates efficiently, regardless of geographic constraints. As remote work continues to grow, the ability to provide effective remote support is becoming an increasingly important skill for IT professionals.

Cybersecurity plays a significant role in IT support operations. Service desk analysts must ensure that users adhere to security policies and best practices, such as using strong passwords, enabling multi-factor authentication (MFA), and avoiding phishing scams. IT teams are often the first line of defense against cyber threats, as they handle security-related incidents, respond to suspicious activities, and educate users on safe computing practices. Organizations implement access controls, network monitoring, and endpoint security measures to protect sensitive data, and service desk professionals must enforce these policies while assisting users with their daily tasks. A security-aware IT support team helps prevent data breaches and reduces the risk of cyberattacks.

The service desk is not only responsible for troubleshooting and incident resolution but also for proactive IT support. Preventative maintenance, system monitoring, and software updates help reduce the occurrence of technical issues before they impact users. Many IT departments use automated monitoring tools that detect potential failures, allowing them to address problems before they escalate. Patch management ensures that operating systems and applications remain up to date, minimizing vulnerabilities that could be exploited by attackers. By focusing on both reactive and proactive support, IT teams create a more stable and reliable technology environment for their organizations.

Collaboration between IT support teams and other departments is essential for maintaining seamless operations. Service desk analysts frequently interact with network administrators, software developers, cybersecurity professionals, and business stakeholders to resolve issues and improve IT services. A strong relationship between IT and business teams ensures that technology aligns with organizational goals and enhances overall productivity. Clear communication and well-defined processes allow IT support teams to address technical challenges efficiently while contributing to the organization's long-term success.

IT support and service desk operations continue to evolve as technology advances. The rise of artificial intelligence, automation, and self-service solutions is transforming the way IT teams provide support. AI-powered chatbots and virtual assistants can handle common user inquiries, allowing service desk analysts to focus on more complex tasks. Self-service portals enable users to access troubleshooting guides, FAQs, and knowledge bases to resolve minor issues independently. While automation improves efficiency, human expertise remains irreplaceable, especially for handling critical incidents and providing personalized assistance.

A career in IT support and service desk operations offers numerous opportunities for growth and specialization. Many professionals use the service desk as a stepping stone to more advanced roles in system administration, network engineering, cybersecurity, or IT management. The experience gained from troubleshooting diverse technical issues, working with different technologies, and interacting with users provides a strong foundation for career advancement. Those who excel in IT support often develop skills that allow them to move into leadership positions, manage IT projects, or specialize in specific areas of technology.

The service desk plays a vital role in ensuring that organizations operate efficiently by providing technical support, resolving incidents, and implementing best practices for IT service management. With a strong understanding of IT support operations, professionals can contribute to the success of their organizations while building a rewarding career in the ever-evolving field of information technology.

The Importance of Customer Service in IT Support

Customer service is the backbone of IT support. While technical knowledge is crucial for resolving issues, the way an IT professional interacts with users often determines the overall success of the support experience. Many people seeking IT help are frustrated, stressed, or in urgent need of assistance, and how an analyst communicates and responds to their concerns can significantly impact their perception of the IT department. A service desk analyst's ability to provide effective, empathetic, and efficient customer service can turn a negative situation into a positive experience, reinforcing trust in the IT team and improving overall satisfaction within an organization.

IT support is not just about fixing technical issues; it is about helping people. Many end users are not technically skilled, and encountering problems with their devices, software, or network can be intimidating. They rely on the service desk to not only solve their problems but to guide them through the resolution process in a way that is clear and reassuring. Using technical jargon without explanation can confuse users and make them feel alienated. A great IT support professional knows how to simplify technical concepts, break down troubleshooting steps into easy-to-follow instructions, and ensure the user feels supported throughout the process.

Communication skills play a crucial role in delivering excellent customer service in IT support. Service desk analysts must be able to listen carefully to users, ask the right questions, and provide clear and concise answers. Active listening is particularly important because many users may not know how to articulate their problems accurately. By paying attention to the details they provide and asking clarifying questions, an IT analyst can quickly diagnose the issue and take the appropriate steps to resolve it. Miscommunication or assumptions can lead to unnecessary troubleshooting steps, wasted time, and frustration on both sides.

Empathy is another key component of great customer service in IT support. When users experience technical difficulties, it often disrupts their work, causes delays, and adds stress to their day. A service desk analyst who approaches each case with understanding and patience helps create a more positive interaction. A simple acknowledgment of the user's frustration, such as 'I understand how frustrating this must be for you,' can make a significant difference in how the user perceives the support experience. Empathy helps build rapport and reassures users that the IT team genuinely cares about resolving their issues.

Patience is essential when dealing with users who may not have a strong technical background. Some users may struggle to follow troubleshooting steps, may ask the same question multiple times, or may become impatient if the issue is not resolved immediately. A skilled IT support professional remains calm and composed, ensuring that they guide users through the resolution process at a pace that suits them. Rushing through explanations or displaying frustration can damage the relationship between IT and the user community, making users hesitant to seek help in the future.

The ability to maintain a professional and positive attitude in challenging situations is another important aspect of customer service in IT support. Not all users will be polite, and some may be openly frustrated or even rude due to their technical issues. It is crucial for IT professionals to remain professional, avoid taking negative interactions personally, and focus on resolving the problem at hand. A calm and composed demeanor can help de-escalate tense situations and prevent conflicts from escalating further. Often, users will later apologize for their behavior once their issue has been resolved and they recognize the IT analyst's patience and professionalism.

Responsiveness is another major factor in delivering excellent customer service. Users expect timely responses to their issues, especially when the problem is preventing them from completing their work. Service Level Agreements (SLAs) often define the expected response and resolution times for different types of IT issues, but even beyond SLAs, the perception of responsiveness matters. A quick acknowledgment of a user's request, even if an immediate solution is not available, reassures them that their issue is being addressed. Following up with users to update them on the status of their request also demonstrates that their concerns are taken seriously.

Consistency in customer service is essential for maintaining a reliable IT support experience. Users should feel confident that whenever they contact the service desk, they will receive the same level of professionalism, expertise, and courtesy. A lack of consistency can lead to frustration, as users may receive excellent support one day but struggle with an unhelpful interaction another day. IT teams should establish best practices and training programs to ensure that all analysts provide a consistent and high-quality level of support.

Customer service in IT support also involves educating users. While resolving issues is the primary focus, providing guidance on how to prevent future problems can be equally valuable. When a user encounters a recurring issue, instead of simply fixing it, a great IT support professional will take the time to explain why it happens and what steps the user can take to avoid it in the future. Educating users empowers them to handle minor technical issues independently, reducing the overall support workload and improving efficiency.

Proactive support is another way that excellent customer service enhances IT operations. Instead of waiting for users to encounter problems, IT teams can anticipate potential issues and address them before they become major disruptions. This can include sending out warnings about known issues, providing regular system updates, and offering training sessions on common IT concerns. When users see that IT support is actively working to prevent problems rather than just reacting to them, they develop greater trust and appreciation for the service desk team.

The reputation of the IT department within an organization is heavily influenced by the level of customer service it provides. A service desk that is known for being helpful, responsive, and professional will be seen as an asset to the company. Employees will be more likely to reach out for assistance when needed, leading to quicker issue resolution and improved overall efficiency. Conversely, if IT support is perceived as unhelpful, slow, or difficult to work with, users may try to find workarounds, leading to security risks, productivity loss, and unnecessary complications.

Customer service in IT support is not just about solving technical problems—it is about creating a positive experience for users, fostering trust in the IT department, and ensuring that technology remains a tool that enables productivity rather than a source of frustration. The best IT support professionals understand that their role goes beyond troubleshooting; they are also communicators, educators, and problem-solvers who make a meaningful impact on the daily operations of their organizations.

Essential Technical Skills for a Helpdesk Analyst

A helpdesk analyst must possess a strong foundation of technical skills to effectively diagnose, troubleshoot, and resolve a wide range of IT-related issues. While customer service and communication are critical components of the role, technical expertise allows an analyst to provide accurate and efficient solutions. The ability to navigate operating systems, understand network configurations, troubleshoot hardware and software problems, and manage security protocols is essential for ensuring seamless IT support. As technology evolves, helpdesk analysts must continuously expand their knowledge to keep up with new tools, systems, and best practices.

One of the most fundamental technical skills required for a helpdesk analyst is proficiency in operating systems. A significant portion of IT support involves assisting users with issues related to Windows, macOS, and Linux environments. Helpdesk analysts must be familiar with installing, configuring, and troubleshooting these operating systems, as well as understanding user account management, file permissions, and system settings. Many organizations rely on Windows-based infrastructures, making knowledge of Windows troubleshooting techniques, such as managing the registry, resolving driver conflicts, and utilizing system recovery options, particularly valuable. Mac users often require assistance with Finder, Terminal commands, and software compatibility, while Linux users may need help navigating different distributions, package managers, and command-line tools.

Hardware troubleshooting is another key skill for a helpdesk analyst. Computers, printers, monitors, and peripherals are prone to malfunctions, and an analyst must be able to diagnose and resolve hardware-related issues. This includes identifying faulty RAM, replacing hard drives, resolving power supply problems, and ensuring proper connectivity between devices. Knowledge of BIOS and UEFI settings, boot sequence configurations, and basic hardware upgrades is essential. Additionally, understanding how to troubleshoot peripherals such as keyboards, mice, external hard drives, and docking stations can prevent unnecessary device replacements and improve user productivity.

Networking knowledge is crucial for resolving connectivity issues. Helpdesk analysts must understand how networks function, including IP addressing, DNS, DHCP, and subnetting. Many user issues stem from network misconfigurations, slow internet connections, or problems accessing shared resources. Being able to diagnose and troubleshoot network connectivity issues, reset routers and modems, configure VPN connections, and interpret network diagnostic tools such as ping, tracert, and ipconfig allows analysts to restore connectivity quickly. Additionally, familiarity with Wi-Fi troubleshooting, SSID configurations, and basic firewall settings is necessary for supporting both home and enterprise network environments.

Email support is a common request for helpdesk analysts, as email remains one of the primary communication tools in most organizations. Analysts must be familiar with setting up, configuring, and troubleshooting email clients such as Microsoft Outlook, Mozilla Thunderbird, and Apple Mail. Understanding email protocols such as SMTP, IMAP, and POP3 is necessary for resolving synchronization issues, undelivered emails, and account authentication problems. Many organizations use cloud-based email services like Microsoft 365 or Google Workspace, requiring analysts to manage user accounts, troubleshoot webmail access, and enforce security policies such as multi-factor authentication (MFA).

A helpdesk analyst must also have experience working with Active Directory (AD) and other directory services. Many companies use Active Directory for user authentication, group policy enforcement, and resource access management. Analysts must be able to create, modify, and disable user accounts, reset passwords, assign permissions, and troubleshoot authentication issues. Understanding group policies, organizational units, and access control lists (ACLs) ensures that users have the necessary permissions while maintaining security and compliance with company policies.

Remote desktop support is an essential skill, especially with the increase in remote work environments. Helpdesk analysts must be proficient in using remote access tools such as Microsoft Remote Desktop, AnyDesk, TeamViewer, and Chrome Remote Desktop. These tools allow analysts to troubleshoot issues on a user's machine without requiring physical access. Understanding how to establish remote connections, resolve session timeouts, and configure permissions for remote assistance is crucial for providing timely support to off-site employees.

Basic scripting and automation knowledge can significantly enhance an analyst's efficiency. Many IT support tasks, such as resetting passwords, creating user accounts, and deploying software updates, can be automated using PowerShell, Bash, or Python scripts. Learning how to write simple scripts for repetitive tasks reduces manual effort, minimizes errors, and speeds up resolution times. Additionally, knowledge of batch scripting and automation tools like SCCM (System Center Configuration Manager) or Ansible can be useful in larger IT environments.

Cybersecurity awareness is an important aspect of IT support. Helpdesk analysts are often the first line of defense against security threats such as phishing attacks, malware infections, and unauthorized access attempts. Analysts must be able to recognize suspicious activity, assist users in identifying phishing emails, enforce password policies, and educate employees on safe computing practices. Familiarity with antivirus software, endpoint security tools, and basic security auditing techniques is essential for maintaining a secure IT environment.

Troubleshooting software and application issues is another core responsibility of a helpdesk analyst. Many organizations use a variety of productivity tools, business applications, and industry-specific software that require support. Analysts must be able to diagnose software crashes, resolve compatibility issues, and reinstall or update applications as needed. Knowledge of software licensing, activation keys, and digital rights management (DRM) ensures that applications function properly while complying with legal and organizational requirements.

Understanding IT service management (ITSM) and ticketing systems is critical for efficiently handling support requests. Helpdesk analysts rely on ITSM platforms such as ServiceNow, Jira Service Management, Freshdesk, or Zendesk to log, track, and resolve user issues. Analysts must know how to categorize incidents, assign priority levels, document troubleshooting steps, and escalate issues when necessary. Proper documentation not only helps in resolving current problems but also contributes to knowledge bases that assist in future troubleshooting.

Virtualization and cloud computing knowledge are becoming increasingly relevant in IT support. Many organizations use virtual machines (VMs) and cloud-based services such as Microsoft Azure, Amazon Web Services (AWS), and Google Cloud. Helpdesk analysts must understand how to configure, deploy, and troubleshoot virtual environments, as well as assist users with cloud storage, file synchronization, and software-as-a-service (SaaS) applications. As businesses continue migrating to the cloud, analysts with cloud support experience will be in high demand.

A successful helpdesk analyst must possess a diverse set of technical skills to effectively address user issues and maintain IT operations. The ability to troubleshoot operating systems, hardware, networking, email, security, and applications is essential for providing efficient and reliable support. As technology continues to evolve, analysts must stay updated with emerging trends, new tools, and best practices to remain effective in their roles. The foundation of technical expertise not only enables analysts to resolve issues efficiently but also prepares them for career advancement in the IT industry.

Soft Skills: Communication and Empathy

Technical knowledge is undoubtedly crucial for a helpdesk analyst, but without strong soft skills, even the most technically proficient professional will struggle to provide effective support. Among the most important soft skills in IT support are communication and empathy. These two skills allow analysts to connect with users, understand their issues, and guide them toward solutions in a way that is clear, supportive, and reassuring. Many users who seek IT support are frustrated, confused, or even anxious about their technical problems. The way an analyst communicates and empathizes with them can determine whether the interaction is a positive or negative experience. Developing these skills not only improves customer satisfaction but also enhances teamwork, efficiency, and the overall reputation of the IT department.

Communication is at the heart of IT support. Every interaction between a helpdesk analyst and a user involves some level of communication, whether through email, phone calls, live chat, or in-person conversations. The ability to explain technical concepts in a simple and understandable way is one of the most valuable skills an analyst can possess. Many users have limited technical knowledge, and overly complex explanations can lead to confusion, frustration, and miscommunication. A great helpdesk analyst knows how to adapt their language based on the user's level of understanding, avoiding jargon when speaking to non-technical users while still being precise when interacting with more knowledgeable individuals.

Listening is just as important as speaking in IT support. Active listening allows analysts to fully understand the user's problem before jumping into a solution. Users may not always describe their issues in technical terms, and some may struggle to explain what went wrong. A skilled analyst pays close attention to the details, asks clarifying questions, and paraphrases the problem to ensure they have accurately understood the issue. Poor listening can lead to incorrect assumptions, unnecessary troubleshooting steps, and wasted time. By truly listening to users, analysts can diagnose problems more efficiently and build trust in the process.

Empathy is another critical soft skill that distinguishes an exceptional helpdesk analyst from an average one. Many users who contact the service desk are not just dealing with a technical problem—they may also be under pressure to meet a deadline, worried about losing important data, or frustrated by repeated issues. A lack of empathy can make users feel like they are just another ticket in a queue rather than individuals with real concerns. When an analyst acknowledges the user's frustration and reassures them that their issue is important, it can immediately de-escalate tension and create a more cooperative interaction. Simple statements like, 'I understand how frustrating this must be for you,' or 'I appreciate your patience while we work on this,' can go a long way in making users feel heard and valued.

The tone of voice in both verbal and written communication plays a significant role in how a message is received. A monotone or rushed response can make users feel like their concerns are not taken seriously, while a patient and friendly tone can reassure them that they are in good hands. When communicating via email or chat, helpdesk analysts must be mindful of how their words come across. Text-based communication lacks tone and body language, making it easy for messages to be misinterpreted. Adding a friendly greeting, using clear and polite language, and ensuring instructions are well-structured can help create a positive experience for the user.

Managing user expectations is another important aspect of communication in IT support. Users often want immediate solutions, but not all problems can be resolved instantly. A helpdesk analyst must be able to provide realistic timelines without making promises they cannot keep. If a problem requires escalation or additional time to investigate, the user should be informed of the next steps and given an estimated time frame for resolution. Regular updates, even if there is no new information, show users that their issue has not been forgotten and that the IT team is actively working on a solution. Clear and transparent communication helps prevent frustration and ensures that users remain informed throughout the process.

Handling difficult users is a challenge that every helpdesk analyst will face at some point. Some users may be impatient, rude, or even aggressive due to their frustration with a technical issue. A professional analyst remains calm, does not take negativity personally, and focuses on finding a solution rather than engaging in conflict. Responding with patience and maintaining a composed demeanor can help de-escalate tense situations. If a user becomes unreasonable, setting polite but firm boundaries while continuing to assist them professionally is the best approach. Empathy in these situations is key—understanding that the user's frustration is likely due to their circumstances rather than a personal attack can help analysts remain composed and focused on resolution.

Collaboration is another area where communication and empathy play a crucial role. Helpdesk analysts often work as part of a larger IT team, coordinating with other departments such as network administrators, security teams, and software developers. Effective communication within the team ensures that issues are escalated appropriately, knowledge is shared, and solutions are implemented efficiently. A lack of clear communication can result in misunderstandings, duplicate efforts, or unresolved issues falling through the cracks. An empathetic approach to teamwork fosters a positive work environment where colleagues support each other and work together toward common goals.

Cultural awareness and adaptability are becoming increasingly important as IT support teams often assist users from diverse backgrounds, locations, and levels of technical expertise. Being able to adjust communication styles to accommodate different cultural expectations and individual preferences helps create a more inclusive and effective support experience. Some users may prefer detailed step-by-step explanations, while others may only need a quick answer. Understanding these differences and adjusting communication accordingly ensures that users receive the level of support that best suits their needs.

Soft skills like communication and empathy are what separate a good helpdesk analyst from a great one. The ability to actively listen, explain technical concepts clearly, demonstrate patience, and show genuine concern for users' challenges creates a support experience that is both effective and positive. These skills not only improve interactions with users but also strengthen teamwork, enhance workplace relationships, and contribute to career growth in the IT industry. Developing and refining these abilities is just as important as staying updated with technical knowledge, as they play a vital role in providing high-quality IT support and building trust between the IT team and the users they assist.

Ticketing Systems: How to Log and Manage Incidents

A ticketing system is the backbone of any organized IT support operation. It serves as a centralized platform for tracking, managing, and resolving user-reported incidents and service requests. Without a structured system in place, IT teams would struggle to maintain efficiency, prioritize tasks, and ensure that no issue goes unresolved. Helpdesk analysts rely on ticketing systems to document problems, communicate with users, escalate issues when necessary, and maintain a record of past incidents. Understanding how to effectively log and manage incidents within a ticketing system is crucial for delivering high-quality IT support and maintaining smooth operations.

Logging an incident correctly is the first step in ensuring a problem is resolved efficiently. When a user reports an issue, whether through a phone call, email, chat, or self-service portal, the helpdesk analyst must gather as much relevant information as possible. The details included in a ticket determine how quickly and accurately the issue can be diagnosed. Essential information typically includes the user's name, contact details, device or system affected, a clear description of the problem, error messages received, and any troubleshooting steps the user may have already attempted. Providing insufficient or vague details in a ticket can lead to delays, unnecessary back-and-forth communication, and an increased resolution time.

Categorization is another key aspect of logging an incident. Most ticketing systems allow analysts to classify tickets based on issue type, priority, and affected services. Proper categorization helps IT teams prioritize their workload and assign tickets to the appropriate support personnel. For example, a printer malfunction may be classified under 'hardware issues,' while an email login problem would fall under 'account access.' Some organizations use predefined categories and subcategories to streamline this process, ensuring that incidents are consistently logged in a structured manner. Correct categorization also enables reporting and analytics, allowing IT managers to identify trends, recurring issues, and areas that require improvement.

Once an incident is logged and categorized, assigning the correct priority level is essential. Not all issues have the same urgency, and ticketing systems typically use priority levels such as low, medium, high, and critical to distinguish between different levels of impact. A password reset request may be considered low priority, while a network outage affecting an entire office would be classified as critical. Many organizations define Service Level Agreements (SLAs) that dictate how quickly each priority level must be addressed. SLAs help set user expectations and ensure that critical issues are resolved within an acceptable timeframe. Helpdesk analysts must be able to assess the urgency of each incident and assign priority accordingly, preventing minor issues from delaying the resolution of more severe problems.

Managing open tickets effectively requires continuous tracking and updates. Once a ticket has been logged, it should not be left unattended or unresolved for long periods. Analysts must regularly review their queue of open tickets, update users on progress, and follow up on any necessary actions. Many ticketing systems provide automation features that remind analysts to check on unresolved tickets, ensuring that nothing is overlooked. Keeping users informed about the status of their requests builds trust in the IT support process and reduces frustration, even when an immediate solution is not available.

Communication within a ticketing system plays a significant role in managing incidents. Analysts must document all troubleshooting steps taken, conversations with users, and any changes made to the affected system. Clear and detailed documentation ensures that if another analyst needs to take over the case, they can quickly understand what has already been done without having to start from scratch. Good documentation also provides historical reference for recurring issues, allowing IT teams to develop long-term solutions rather than repeatedly addressing the same problem. Additionally, well-documented tickets serve as a knowledge base for future troubleshooting, helping new analysts learn from past cases.

Escalation is an important aspect of incident management. Not all issues can be resolved at the helpdesk level, and some require specialized expertise. Most IT support teams operate within a tiered structure, with Tier 1 handling basic issues, Tier 2 addressing more complex problems, and Tier 3 dealing with advanced technical challenges. When an analyst encounters an issue beyond their expertise or authority, they must escalate the ticket to the appropriate team. Proper escalation ensures that users receive the correct level of support without unnecessary delays. However, before escalating, analysts should always document their findings and initial troubleshooting steps, so higher-tier teams do not have to repeat work already completed.

Resolution and closure of tickets require careful attention to detail. Once an issue has been resolved, the analyst must confirm with the user that the solution has been effective before marking the ticket as closed. Some ticketing systems include a feedback mechanism that allows users to rate their support experience, providing valuable insights into the quality of service provided. Analysts should also ensure that resolution notes are detailed enough for future reference, particularly for complex or recurring issues. Closing a ticket prematurely without verifying user satisfaction can lead to reopened cases, increased frustration, and a decline in service desk efficiency.

Analytics and reporting features within ticketing systems provide IT teams with valuable data for continuous improvement. By analyzing trends in ticket volume, resolution times, and common issues, IT managers can identify areas that require additional training, resource allocation, or process refinement. Regular reviews of ticketing system data can help organizations proactively address potential problems, improve response times, and enhance overall IT support performance. Many ticketing systems also integrate with knowledge base platforms, allowing IT teams to build a library of solutions that users can access for self-service troubleshooting, reducing the number of repetitive support requests.

Modern ticketing systems often incorporate automation and artificial intelligence to enhance efficiency. Automated workflows can route tickets to the appropriate support personnel based on predefined rules, ensuring that incidents are handled by the right team from the start.

AI-powered chatbots can assist users with common issues, allowing them to find solutions without human intervention. Machine learning algorithms can also analyze ticket data to predict potential problems before they escalate. As technology continues to evolve, helpdesk analysts must familiarize themselves with these advanced features to optimize their workflow and provide faster, more efficient support.

A well-managed ticketing system is the foundation of an effective IT support team. By properly logging, categorizing, prioritizing, and tracking incidents, helpdesk analysts ensure that user issues are addressed in an organized and timely manner. The ability to document troubleshooting steps, escalate issues appropriately, and maintain clear communication with users leads to a smoother and more transparent support process. Ticketing systems not only help analysts manage their workload but also provide organizations with valuable insights into IT performance and areas for improvement. Mastering the use of a ticketing system is essential for any helpdesk analyst seeking to provide high-quality technical support and contribute to the overall efficiency of the IT department.

ITIL Basics: Incident, Problem, and Change Management

The IT Infrastructure Library (ITIL) is a widely adopted framework for IT service management (ITSM) that provides structured best practices for delivering high-quality IT support. Organizations around the world use ITIL to standardize their IT processes, improve efficiency, and ensure that services align with business needs. Among the core components of ITIL, three key areas are essential for helpdesk and service desk analysts: incident management, problem management, and change management. These processes help IT teams maintain stability, reduce downtime, and implement necessary changes without disrupting operations. Understanding how each of these areas functions and how they interconnect is crucial for any IT professional working in a support role.

Incident management is one of the most frequently used processes in ITIL. An incident is any unplanned interruption or reduction in the quality of an IT service. This can range from a minor issue, such as a user being unable to print, to major outages affecting an entire organization. The goal of incident management is to restore normal service operations as quickly as possible while minimizing the impact on business activities. Helpdesk analysts play a crucial role in this process, as they are often the first point of contact when users experience technical difficulties.

The incident management process begins with the logging of an incident in the ticketing system. Analysts must document the issue accurately, including details about the affected system, error messages, and any initial troubleshooting steps taken. Categorization and prioritization are essential steps in incident management, as they help IT teams determine the urgency of an issue and allocate resources accordingly. Low-priority incidents, such as minor software glitches, may be addressed within a standard response time, while high-priority incidents, such as a company-wide email outage, require immediate attention.

Once an incident is logged and prioritized, analysts begin troubleshooting to identify the root cause and implement a solution. This process may involve following predefined scripts, checking knowledge base articles, or escalating the issue to a higher-tier support team. The faster an incident is diagnosed and resolved, the less impact it has on business operations. Effective communication with users is critical during this stage, as keeping them informed about the progress of their issue helps manage expectations and reduces frustration.

If an incident cannot be resolved immediately, temporary workarounds may be implemented to restore functionality while a permanent fix is developed. For example, if a user cannot access their email due to a server issue, an alternative email account or webmail access may be provided until the primary system is restored. Once the incident is resolved, analysts document the solution, close the ticket, and, if necessary, update the knowledge base to assist with future occurrences of the same issue.

Problem management differs from incident management in that it focuses on identifying and eliminating the underlying causes of recurring incidents rather than just addressing individual issues. While incident management aims for quick resolutions, problem management seeks long-term solutions that prevent future disruptions. A problem is defined as the root cause of one or more incidents, and resolving it often requires deeper investigation and analysis.

The problem management process begins with problem detection, which can occur through multiple channels. Recurring incidents reported by users, trends identified in ticketing system analytics, or proactive monitoring of IT infrastructure may all reveal underlying problems that need to be addressed. Once a problem is identified, IT teams conduct a thorough investigation to determine its root cause. This may involve analyzing system logs, replicating issues in a test environment, or consulting with vendors and subject matter experts.

Once the root cause of a problem is identified, IT teams develop a permanent solution, also known as a 'Known Error' resolution. This solution is then tested, documented, and implemented in a controlled manner. If an immediate fix is not possible, workarounds may be documented to help users minimize disruption until a full resolution is available. The problem management process often involves collaboration between different IT teams, including system administrators, network engineers, and software developers, to ensure a comprehensive approach to issue resolution.

Change management is another critical ITIL process that ensures modifications to IT systems and services are implemented in a controlled and systematic manner. Changes can include software updates, hardware upgrades, network modifications, or policy adjustments. Poorly managed changes can introduce new problems, cause system outages, and disrupt business operations. The change management process minimizes risks by ensuring that all changes are carefully planned, tested, and approved before implementation.

The change management process begins with a change request, which documents the details of the proposed modification, the reason for the change, and the potential impact on IT services. Change requests are categorized based on their complexity and level of risk. Low-risk changes, such as minor software patches, may follow a streamlined approval process, while high-risk changes, such as a data center migration, require thorough planning and multiple levels of approval.

Once a change request is submitted, it is reviewed by a Change Advisory Board (CAB), which consists of IT managers, business stakeholders, and subject matter experts. The CAB evaluates the potential risks and benefits of the proposed change and determines whether it should proceed. If approved, the change is scheduled for implementation during a designated maintenance window to minimize disruption to users.

Before a change is implemented, it is tested in a controlled environment to ensure that it does not introduce unexpected issues. Testing may involve running simulations, verifying compatibility with existing systems, and assessing performance impacts. If the test results are satisfactory, the change is deployed according to the implementation plan. Throughout this process, communication with end users is essential, especially if the change affects their workflow or requires them to take specific actions.

After the change is implemented, IT teams monitor its effects to ensure that it functions as intended. If any issues arise, a rollback plan is executed to restore systems to their previous state. Once the change is confirmed to be successful, final documentation is completed, and the change request is closed. Lessons learned from the change implementation process may be documented to improve future change management efforts.

Incident management, problem management, and change management are interconnected processes that contribute to a stable and efficient IT environment. Effective incident management ensures quick resolution of technical issues, problem management addresses root causes to prevent recurring incidents, and change management ensures that IT modifications are implemented without disrupting operations. Helpdesk analysts who understand these ITIL processes can provide better support, reduce system downtime, and contribute to the overall improvement of IT service delivery within their organization.

Troubleshooting Methodologies and Best Practices

Troubleshooting is one of the most fundamental skills required for a helpdesk analyst. Every day, analysts encounter a variety of technical issues, ranging from simple software malfunctions to complex network failures. Effective troubleshooting is not about randomly trying different solutions until something works—it requires a structured, logical approach to diagnosing and resolving problems efficiently. The ability to systematically investigate an issue, identify its root cause, and apply an appropriate fix is what separates an average IT support professional from an exceptional one. By following established troubleshooting methodologies and best practices, helpdesk analysts can improve their efficiency, reduce resolution times, and ensure a consistent approach to technical support.

One of the most commonly used troubleshooting methodologies is the six-step troubleshooting process, which provides a structured way to diagnose and resolve IT issues. The first step in this process is identifying the problem. This involves gathering information from the user, asking detailed questions, and observing any error messages or symptoms. Users may not always describe their issues accurately, so it is crucial for the analyst to clarify what the problem is, when it started occurring, and whether any changes were made to the system before the issue appeared. Many problems can be quickly diagnosed simply by understanding the circumstances under which they occur.

The second step is establishing a theory of probable cause. At this stage, the helpdesk analyst should consider all possible explanations for the issue, starting with the most common and simplest causes. It is a best practice to begin troubleshooting with the least complex and least disruptive potential solutions. For example, if a user reports that their computer will not turn on, the first step should be checking if the power cable is properly connected before considering more advanced troubleshooting steps like inspecting the power supply unit.

Once a potential cause has been identified, the next step is testing the theory to determine whether it is correct. This can involve performing diagnostic tests, replicating the issue in a controlled environment, or making a small, reversible change to see if it has an impact. If the initial theory is incorrect, the analyst should revisit their list of possible causes and test alternative explanations until the root cause is found. Patience and methodical thinking are essential during this stage, as jumping to conclusions or making hasty changes can sometimes worsen the issue.

After identifying the root cause, the fourth step is developing and implementing a solution. The analyst should choose the most effective fix while considering factors such as downtime, user impact, and security. Some solutions may require approval from higher-level IT teams or management, especially if they involve significant changes to system settings, security policies, or network configurations. If multiple solutions exist, the analyst should evaluate which one is the most practical and sustainable.

The fifth step is verifying full system functionality and, if applicable, implementing preventative measures to ensure the issue does not reoccur. Simply fixing the problem is not enough—the analyst must test the affected system to confirm that everything is working correctly. For example, if an email client was unable to send messages, the analyst should send a test email and confirm that the user can receive replies before closing the ticket. Additionally, if a recurring issue was resolved, the analyst should consider updating documentation or educating users on best practices to prevent the same problem in the future.

The final step in the troubleshooting process is documenting findings, actions, and outcomes. Proper documentation is essential for knowledge sharing, tracking recurring problems, and improving future troubleshooting efforts. Detailed records of the issue, the steps taken to resolve it, and the final solution should be logged in the ticketing system. This helps other analysts who may encounter similar issues in the future and ensures continuity in case the problem needs to be revisited later.

Aside from structured troubleshooting methodologies, there are several best practices that every helpdesk analyst should follow to improve their troubleshooting effectiveness. One of the most important principles is the 'divide and conquer' approach, which involves isolating different components of a system to identify the source of the problem. For example, if a user cannot connect to the internet, the analyst should first determine whether the issue is with the individual device, the local network, or the internet service provider. By systematically eliminating possible causes, analysts can narrow down the scope of the issue and focus on the most likely solution.

Another best practice is replicating the issue whenever possible. If an analyst can reproduce an error on their own system or in a controlled test environment, it provides valuable insights into the problem. This can help determine whether the issue is related to a specific configuration, software version, or network condition. When an issue is not easily replicable, the analyst should gather as much detailed information from the user as possible to simulate similar conditions.

Using logical troubleshooting trees and flowcharts is another effective strategy for resolving technical problems efficiently. Many organizations develop structured troubleshooting guides that outline step-by-step procedures for diagnosing common issues. These guides help ensure consistency in troubleshooting efforts and provide a reference for analysts who may be unfamiliar with a particular problem. Even without formal troubleshooting trees, analysts should develop their own logical sequences for addressing different types of issues.

Avoiding unnecessary changes is another critical best practice. Making multiple changes at once can complicate troubleshooting efforts, as it becomes difficult to determine which action actually resolved the problem. Whenever possible, analysts should make one change at a time, test the results, and document their observations before proceeding to additional troubleshooting steps. This controlled approach prevents unintended consequences and reduces the risk of introducing new problems.

Remaining calm and patient under pressure is an essential skill for helpdesk analysts, especially when dealing with urgent or high-priority incidents. Users experiencing major technical issues may be anxious or frustrated, and it is the analyst's responsibility to remain professional and focused on finding a solution. Rushing through troubleshooting steps can lead to mistakes, so maintaining a clear and logical approach is crucial for effective problem resolution.

Leveraging available tools and resources is another best practice that can significantly improve troubleshooting efficiency. Many IT departments provide access to diagnostic utilities, log files, remote desktop tools, and vendor documentation that can help analysts quickly identify issues. Online forums, knowledge bases, and support communities can also provide valuable insights, especially when dealing with unfamiliar problems. Knowing where to find reliable information is just as important as having technical knowledge.

Troubleshooting is an essential skill that requires a combination of structured methodologies, logical thinking, and adherence to best practices. By following a systematic approach, documenting findings, and continuously improving their problem-solving techniques, helpdesk analysts can ensure that they resolve technical issues efficiently while maintaining a high level of service quality. The ability to troubleshoot effectively not only enhances an analyst's ability to resolve issues quickly but also contributes to the overall efficiency and success of the IT support team.

Remote Support Tools and Techniques

Remote support has become an essential component of IT service desks, enabling analysts to troubleshoot and resolve issues without needing to be physically present with the user. As organizations adopt hybrid work environments and rely on distributed teams, remote support tools and techniques allow IT professionals to provide assistance across different locations, time zones, and devices. A helpdesk analyst must be proficient in using a variety of remote support solutions, understand the security implications of remote access, and develop effective communication strategies to assist users who may have limited technical expertise. Mastering these tools and techniques ensures that support teams can provide timely, efficient, and secure assistance, minimizing downtime and improving user satisfaction.

One of the primary remote support tools used in IT service desks is remote desktop software, which allows analysts to access a user's device over the internet or internal network. Applications like Microsoft Remote Desktop, AnyDesk, TeamViewer, Chrome Remote Desktop, and Splashtop enable analysts to view and control the user's screen, perform administrative tasks, and troubleshoot issues as if they were physically at the workstation. These tools streamline IT support by eliminating the need for users to describe complex issues verbally, allowing analysts to directly observe and resolve problems. Many of these applications offer features such as file transfer, session recording, and chat functionality, enhancing collaboration between the analyst and the user.

Virtual Private Network (VPN) access is another crucial component of remote support, especially when assisting employees working from home or traveling. Many corporate environments require VPN connections for secure access to internal systems, shared drives, and enterprise applications. Helpdesk analysts must be familiar with common VPN solutions such as Cisco AnyConnect, OpenVPN, and Palo Alto GlobalProtect. Understanding how to configure VPN settings, troubleshoot connectivity issues, and guide users through authentication processes is essential for maintaining secure and reliable remote work environments.

Another key remote support technique involves secure authentication and access control. Since remote access can introduce security vulnerabilities, IT teams implement authentication measures such as multi-factor authentication (MFA), encrypted sessions, and role-based access controls to ensure that only authorized personnel can remotely access user devices. Analysts must follow strict security protocols, ensuring that they obtain explicit user permission before initiating remote sessions and verify the identity of the individual requesting support. Unauthorized access can lead to data breaches or compromise sensitive information, making security awareness a critical aspect of remote troubleshooting.

Many remote support scenarios involve guiding users through troubleshooting steps without direct access to their devices. Not all organizations permit remote desktop control due to security policies or regulatory compliance requirements. In such cases, analysts must rely on clear and effective communication to walk users through diagnostic procedures, command-line instructions, or software configurations. Tools such as Microsoft Quick Assist, Google Meet screen sharing, and Zoom remote control features allow analysts to provide visual guidance while the user performs necessary actions. Developing the ability to explain technical steps in a simple and patient manner is crucial when users lack IT expertise.

Cloud-based IT support platforms also play a significant role in remote troubleshooting. Solutions like Microsoft Intune, Google Workspace Admin Console, and Jamf Pro allow IT teams to manage devices, push software updates, enforce security policies, and monitor system performance remotely. These tools are especially valuable in large-scale IT environments where manual intervention for every individual issue is impractical. Analysts can use cloud-based management consoles to reset user passwords, configure security settings, and deploy patches without requiring physical access to the endpoint device.

Another essential remote support technique is using system logs and diagnostic tools to identify and resolve issues. Many remote desktop applications include built-in diagnostic tools that allow analysts to check system performance, network connectivity, and application errors. Windows Event Viewer, macOS Console, and Linux syslogs provide valuable insights into system behavior, helping analysts determine the root cause of problems. Network diagnostic commands like ping, tracert, ipconfig, and netstat assist in troubleshooting connectivity issues, ensuring that users can access internal and external resources without disruption.

Remote software deployment and patch management is another important aspect of IT support. Ensuring that all devices have the latest software updates and security patches reduces vulnerabilities and improves performance. Remote management solutions such as Microsoft Endpoint Configuration Manager (SCCM), PDQ Deploy, and NinjaOne allow IT teams to install software, apply patches, and manage system configurations from a centralized console. Helpdesk analysts must be familiar with these tools and understand how to schedule deployments to minimize downtime and prevent disruptions to business operations.

One of the challenges of remote support is handling complex hardware issues that cannot be resolved through software interventions alone. While remote tools can diagnose driver failures, device malfunctions, and system crashes, some problems require physical troubleshooting. In such cases, analysts must determine whether the issue can be temporarily mitigated through a workaround or if the user needs to visit an IT support center or receive replacement hardware. Proper documentation and clear communication are vital to ensuring that users understand the next steps and minimize disruptions to their workflow.

User training and self-service options also enhance the effectiveness of remote support. Providing users with access to a well-maintained knowledge base, instructional videos, and step-by-step troubleshooting guides empowers them to resolve common issues independently. Many organizations integrate self-service portals with their ticketing systems, allowing users to reset passwords, install approved software, and check system status updates without needing direct assistance. Helpdesk analysts should actively contribute to these knowledge bases by documenting recurring issues and creating easy-to-follow resolutions for users.

An often overlooked but critical remote support technique is maintaining professionalism and user confidence. Many users feel uncomfortable granting remote access to their devices, especially when dealing with sensitive data. Helpdesk analysts must establish trust by clearly explaining the purpose of the remote session, seeking explicit consent before making changes, and reassuring users that their privacy is respected. Maintaining transparency throughout the troubleshooting process, explaining each step as it is performed, and confirming resolution with the user before ending the session helps foster positive interactions and improves the overall support experience.

Time management and multitasking play a crucial role in remote support efficiency. Analysts often handle multiple tickets simultaneously, requiring them to prioritize urgent issues while ensuring that all requests receive timely responses. Effective use of ticketing systems, automation tools, and collaboration platforms like Microsoft Teams or Slack allows IT teams to streamline communication and manage workloads efficiently. Balancing responsiveness with thorough troubleshooting ensures that users receive prompt assistance without compromising the quality of support.

Remote support tools and techniques are indispensable for modern IT service desks, enabling analysts to assist users across different locations while maintaining security, efficiency, and professionalism. As organizations continue to adopt remote and hybrid work environments, IT professionals must stay updated on emerging remote support technologies and best practices to provide seamless, effective assistance. Mastering these skills ensures that helpdesk analysts can troubleshoot issues effectively, maintain system reliability, and enhance the overall IT support experience for users regardless of their physical location.

Password Resets and Account Management

Password resets and account management are among the most common tasks handled by helpdesk analysts. A large percentage of IT support requests involve users who have forgotten their passwords, locked themselves out of their accounts, or need access to new systems. While password resets may seem like a simple task, improper handling can lead to security vulnerabilities, compliance issues, and frustration for both users and IT staff. Effective account management requires not only resetting passwords but also ensuring that authentication processes are secure, accounts are properly configured, and access controls are enforced according to organizational policies. A well-structured approach to password management enhances security while maintaining efficiency and user satisfaction.

A password reset request typically occurs when a user is unable to log into their system, email account, or a specific application. Many organizations implement self-service password reset (SSPR) portals that allow users to regain access without contacting the helpdesk. These portals use identity verification methods such as multi-factor authentication (MFA), security questions, or SMS/email verification codes to confirm the user's identity before allowing them to reset their password. However, not all users are familiar with these systems, and many will still call the helpdesk for assistance. It is the responsibility of the helpdesk analyst to guide them through the reset process while ensuring that proper security measures are followed.

When handling a password reset manually, verifying the user's identity is a critical step. Helpdesk analysts should never reset passwords without confirming that the request is coming from the legitimate account owner. Organizations typically use verification methods such as confirming personal details, checking user ID badges, or requiring approval from a manager before proceeding with a reset. If an unauthorized individual gains access to an account due to a weak verification process, it could result in data breaches, identity theft, or malicious activities within the organization. Analysts must remain vigilant and follow established security protocols to prevent unauthorized access.

Once the user's identity has been verified, the analyst can proceed with resetting the password. Many organizations use centralized account management tools such as Active Directory (AD) for Windows environments or LDAP for managing authentication across different systems. In an Active Directory environment, analysts use tools like the Active Directory Users and Computers (ADUC) console or PowerShell commands to reset passwords, unlock accounts, and enforce security policies. If the account is locked due to too many failed login attempts, the analyst can unlock it while advising the user on best practices to avoid repeated lockouts. Some systems enforce password history policies, preventing users from reusing previous passwords, which can sometimes lead to additional support requests when users attempt to reset their passwords to something familiar.

Account management extends beyond just resetting passwords. Helpdesk analysts are often responsible for creating, modifying, and disabling user accounts based on business needs. When a new employee joins an organization, they require accounts for corporate email, enterprise applications, network access, and cloud-based services such as Microsoft 365, Google Workspace, or VPN systems. IT teams follow onboarding procedures to ensure that the new employee has the necessary permissions and access to essential resources. Analysts must be familiar with provisioning tools that automate account creation while ensuring that access rights are granted according to the user's role.

Access control is a fundamental part of account management. Organizations enforce the principle of least privilege (PoLP) to minimize security risks by ensuring that users only have access to the systems and data they need for their specific job functions. Helpdesk analysts play a key role in managing these permissions, often working with role-based access control (RBAC) systems to assign appropriate user roles. When a user requires additional access, the request is typically reviewed by IT security teams or department managers before being granted. Analysts must ensure that all access requests follow proper approval workflows to prevent unauthorized access to sensitive systems.

Another important aspect of account management is handling departing employees and contractors. When an employee leaves an organization, their accounts must be promptly disabled or deactivated to prevent unauthorized access. Failure to properly manage offboarding processes can leave systems vulnerable to security breaches if former employees retain access to company data. IT teams typically follow predefined offboarding procedures, which may include disabling Active Directory accounts, revoking VPN access, collecting company-owned devices, and ensuring email forwarding is configured appropriately. Some companies also implement data retention policies, preserving email accounts for a specific period after an employee departs.

Password security policies play a crucial role in maintaining account security. Organizations enforce password complexity requirements to ensure that users create strong passwords resistant to brute-force attacks. These policies often include minimum length requirements, a mix of uppercase and lowercase letters, numbers, special characters, and password expiration intervals. While enforcing password security is necessary, frequent forced password changes can frustrate users and lead to poor password management habits, such as writing passwords down or reusing similar variations. Many organizations have moved away from frequent password expiration policies in favor of longer passphrases and multi-factor authentication for enhanced security.

Multi-factor authentication (MFA) is an increasingly common security measure that helps protect accounts from unauthorized access. MFA requires users to provide an additional verification factor beyond just a password, such as a one-time password (OTP) sent via SMS or email, a mobile authentication app like Google Authenticator or Microsoft Authenticator, or biometric authentication methods such as fingerprint or facial recognition. Helpdesk analysts often assist users with setting up and troubleshooting MFA-related issues, including lost authentication devices or expired authentication tokens. Organizations may also implement single sign-on (SSO) solutions to reduce the number of passwords users need to remember while maintaining strong security controls.

Social engineering attacks, such as phishing, pose a significant threat to account security. Attackers often attempt to trick users into revealing their login credentials through fake emails, phone calls, or fraudulent websites. Helpdesk analysts must be aware of these threats and educate users on how to recognize and avoid phishing scams. If a user reports suspicious activity, such as receiving an email requesting their login credentials, analysts should instruct them to change their password immediately and report the incident to IT security teams for further investigation. Analysts should also be cautious when handling password reset requests to avoid falling victim to impersonation attempts by attackers pretending to be legitimate users.

Best practices for account management include keeping accurate documentation of all account changes, maintaining logs of access requests and password resets, and regularly reviewing user permissions. IT teams often perform periodic access audits to ensure that inactive accounts are disabled and that users do not have excessive privileges beyond what is necessary for their role. Many security frameworks, such as ISO 27001, NIST, and SOC 2, require organizations to implement strict access control measures and auditing processes to maintain compliance.

Password resets and account management are critical functions of IT support, impacting both security and operational efficiency. Helpdesk analysts must balance the need for quick and efficient support with the responsibility of maintaining strict security protocols. By following best practices, using the right tools, and enforcing strong authentication measures, analysts can ensure that user accounts remain secure while minimizing disruptions to business operations. Properly managed account access and password policies strengthen an organization's overall security posture, reducing the risk of data breaches and unauthorized access.

Network Basics: DNS, DHCP, and IP Addressing

Understanding the fundamentals of networking is essential for any helpdesk analyst, as many IT support issues involve connectivity problems, slow network speeds, or access failures. Among the most critical networking concepts that analysts need to grasp are Domain Name System (DNS), Dynamic Host Configuration Protocol (DHCP), and IP addressing. These components form the foundation of modern network communications, ensuring that devices can connect to each other and access the necessary resources efficiently. A solid grasp of these technologies enables helpdesk analysts to diagnose and troubleshoot network-related issues quickly, improving response times and reducing downtime for users.

DNS, or the Domain Name System, is one of the most fundamental services on the internet and local networks. It functions as a distributed database that translates human-readable domain names, such as www.example.com, into IP addresses that computers use to communicate. Without DNS, users would have to remember complex numerical IP addresses instead of simple domain names when accessing websites and services. When a user types a URL into a web browser, their computer sends a request to a DNS server, which then resolves the domain name to its corresponding IP address. This process allows the browser to establish a connection with the appropriate web server.

DNS resolution involves multiple steps and different types of servers. The process begins with a recursive resolver, which is usually provided by an Internet Service Provider (ISP) or a company's internal network. If the resolver does not already have the IP address cached, it forwards the request to root name servers, which then direct the query to the appropriate top-level domain (TLD) servers based on the domain suffix (.com, .org, .net). Finally, the request reaches an authoritative name server, which provides the correct IP address for the domain. This information is then sent back to the user's device, allowing it to establish a connection.

DNS-related issues are among the most common network problems reported by users. If a user is unable to access a website or a company's internal resources, the issue may be due to a misconfigured DNS setting, a failing DNS server, or a corrupted local DNS cache. Helpdesk analysts can troubleshoot DNS problems by verifying whether the user's device is using the correct DNS server addresses, flushing the DNS cache with commands like ipconfig /flushdns (Windows) or sudo dscacheutil -flushcache (macOS), and testing connectivity using commands such as nslookup or dig. Many organizations use public DNS servers, such as Google's 8.8.8.8 or Cloudflare's 1.1.1.1, to ensure faster and more reliable DNS resolution.

Another critical networking component is DHCP (Dynamic Host Configuration Protocol), which automatically assigns IP addresses and other network settings to devices within a network. Without DHCP, administrators would have to manually configure each device with a unique IP address, a task that would be both time-consuming and prone to errors. DHCP servers ensure that IP addresses are assigned dynamically, preventing conflicts and making network management more efficient.

When a device connects to a network, it sends a DHCP Discover message requesting an IP address. The DHCP server responds with an Offer, providing an available address along with additional settings such as the subnet mask, default gateway, and DNS servers. The client then sends a Request message to confirm its acceptance of the offer, and the DHCP server finalizes the process with an Acknowledgment (ACK). This process, known as DORA (Discover, Offer, Request, Acknowledgment), allows devices to receive their network configurations automatically.

Troubleshooting DHCP issues is a common task for helpdesk analysts, as connectivity problems can arise when a device fails to obtain an IP address from the DHCP server. If a user reports network connectivity issues, checking their IP configuration is a good starting point. Devices that fail to receive a proper IP address from DHCP may default to an Automatic Private IP Addressing (APIPA) address in the 169.254.x.x range. This indicates that the device is unable to reach the DHCP server. Analysts can diagnose DHCP problems by verifying that the DHCP service is running, checking for IP address conflicts, ensuring the network cable or Wi-Fi connection is stable, and renewing the device's lease using the command ipconfig /renew (Windows) or dhclient -r followed by dhclient (Linux/macOS).

IP addressing is another fundamental concept in networking. Every device on a network must have a unique IP address to communicate with other devices. There are two main types of IP addresses: IPv4 and IPv6. IPv4 addresses follow a 32-bit format and are written in dotted decimal notation (e.g., 192.168.1.100). Due to the limited number of available IPv4 addresses, IPv6 was introduced to provide a much larger address space using a 128-bit format written in hexadecimal notation (e.g., 2001:db8::ff00:42:8329).

IPv4 addresses are categorized into different classes (A, B, C, D, and E), with classes A, B, and C being commonly used for network hosts. Within these classes, IP addresses are divided into public and private ranges. Private IP addresses, such as 192.168.x.x, 10.x.x.x, and 172.16.x.x - 172.31.x.x, are reserved for internal networks and require Network Address Translation (NAT) to communicate with public internet resources.

A subnet mask determines which portion of an IP address represents the network and which part identifies the host. Subnetting is used to divide a larger network into smaller, more manageable segments, improving performance and security. Helpdesk analysts should understand subnet masks (e.g., 255.255.255.0) and CIDR notation (e.g., /24) to troubleshoot IP conflicts and network segmentation issues.

One of the most common tools used for troubleshooting IP-related problems is ping, which tests connectivity between a user's device and another network device. Running ping 8.8.8.8 checks whether the device can reach Google's public DNS server, helping analysts determine if the issue is local or internet-related. Other useful commands include tracert (Windows) or traceroute (Linux/macOS), which trace the path packets take to their destination, and netstat, which displays active network connections.

Network issues can arise due to misconfigured DNS settings, DHCP failures, or incorrect IP addressing. A helpdesk analyst must be able to diagnose connectivity problems by checking the IP configuration with ipconfig or ifconfig, ensuring the device is receiving an IP address from DHCP, verifying DNS resolution with nslookup, and testing network reachability with ping or traceroute. A strong understanding of these core networking concepts allows analysts to quickly identify and resolve connectivity issues, ensuring that users can access the resources they need without unnecessary delays.

Hardware Troubleshooting: PCs, Laptops, and Printers

Hardware troubleshooting is a critical skill for a helpdesk analyst, as many support requests involve physical components such as desktop computers, laptops, and printers. Unlike software issues, hardware problems can often be more challenging to diagnose because they involve physical components that may be failing, disconnected, or damaged. A structured approach to troubleshooting ensures that issues are identified efficiently and resolved with minimal downtime. Understanding the common symptoms of hardware failures, knowing how to test and replace components, and following best practices for preventive maintenance are essential for providing effective IT support.

One of the most frequent hardware issues encountered in IT support involves desktop PCs. When a user reports that their computer is not turning on, the analyst must first determine whether the issue is related to power, internal hardware, or peripheral devices. Checking if the power cable is properly connected and testing the outlet with another device helps rule out external power problems. If the power indicator on the PC is off, the power supply unit (PSU) may have failed. A simple way to test this is to use a power supply tester or swap the PSU with a known working one. If the computer powers on but does not boot, the issue could be related to RAM, the motherboard, or the CPU. Removing and reseating the RAM modules, testing with a single module at a time, and checking for motherboard indicator lights can help identify the failing component.

Laptops present unique troubleshooting challenges due to their compact design and integrated components. When a laptop does not turn on, checking the battery and power adapter is the first step. A failing battery may prevent the laptop from powering on even when plugged in. Testing with a different power adapter or removing the battery and running the laptop directly from AC power can determine whether the issue lies with the battery or the charging circuit. If the laptop powers on but has no display, connecting an external monitor can help determine whether the problem is with the laptop's screen or the internal GPU. Other common laptop issues include overheating due to dust buildup in the cooling system, keyboard malfunctions caused by liquid spills, and touchpad failures that may require driver updates or hardware replacements.

Another major area of hardware troubleshooting involves printers, which are often a source of frustration for users and IT teams alike. Printers can experience a wide range of issues, including paper jams, connectivity failures, driver problems, and print quality issues. When a printer fails to respond, the first step is to check its power status and network connectivity. If the printer is connected via USB, trying a different port or cable can rule out physical connection issues. For network printers, verifying the IP address, checking network settings, and pinging the printer from a workstation can help diagnose connectivity problems. Restarting the print spooler service or reinstalling the printer drivers often resolves software-related issues.

Print quality problems, such as streaks or faded prints, may be due to low toner levels, clogged ink nozzles, or worn-out drum units.

Diagnosing hardware failures requires the use of diagnostic tools and built-in system utilities. Many PCs and laptops have built-in BIOS or UEFI diagnostics that can test hardware components before the operating system loads. Running a memory test using Windows Memory Diagnostic or a third-party tool like MemTest86 can help detect faulty RAM. Hard drive failures are another common problem, and checking the drive's health using S.M.A.R.T. (Self-Monitoring, Analysis, and Reporting Technology) tools like CrystalDiskInfo or chkdsk can reveal potential issues. For sudden performance drops, excessive noise, or system crashes, replacing a failing hard drive with a solid-state drive (SSD) can significantly improve performance and reliability.

Overheating is a frequent cause of hardware malfunctions, particularly in laptops and older desktop PCs. Accumulated dust inside the cooling system can block airflow, leading to increased temperatures and thermal throttling. Symptoms of overheating include frequent crashes, sudden shutdowns, and noisy fans running at high speeds. Using a utility such as HWMonitor or Core Temp can help track CPU and GPU temperatures. Cleaning the cooling system with compressed air, replacing thermal paste on the CPU, and ensuring that ventilation is unobstructed can prevent overheating issues. In extreme cases, replacing a failing fan or heatsink may be necessary.

Hardware troubleshooting also involves addressing peripheral device issues. Users often report problems with keyboards, mice, monitors, and external storage devices. If a keyboard or mouse stops working, testing it on another computer can determine whether the issue is with the device itself or the USB port. Wireless peripherals may require battery replacement or re-pairing with the system. Monitors that display a 'no signal' error should be tested with a different cable or on another computer to rule out issues with the display or graphics card. External hard drives and USB flash drives that are not recognized may have corrupted file systems or physical damage, requiring the use of disk recovery tools or professional data recovery services.

Preventive maintenance plays a key role in reducing hardware failures. Regular dust cleaning, checking for loose connections, ensuring proper cable management, and replacing aging components can extend the lifespan of computers and peripherals. IT teams often schedule routine maintenance checks to inspect hardware performance, apply firmware updates, and replace failing parts before they cause significant downtime. Educating users on best practices, such as avoiding overloading power strips, safely ejecting USB drives, and handling laptops carefully, can also prevent common hardware issues.

Proper documentation of hardware troubleshooting steps is essential for IT teams. Keeping detailed records of failed components, replacement parts, and resolved issues helps identify patterns of recurring failures and streamline future troubleshooting efforts. Organizations often maintain asset management databases to track hardware inventory, warranty status, and device lifecycles. This information allows IT departments to plan hardware upgrades, optimize budget allocation, and ensure that aging systems are replaced proactively.

Helpdesk analysts must develop strong problem-solving skills and remain patient when dealing with hardware issues. While some problems can be resolved quickly through simple fixes, others may require in-depth diagnostics and component replacements. Having a structured approach, using the right tools, and maintaining a logical troubleshooting process ensures that hardware failures are addressed efficiently. By mastering these troubleshooting techniques, helpdesk analysts can minimize downtime, improve user productivity, and maintain reliable IT infrastructure.

Software Support: Common Applications and Issues

Software issues are among the most frequent problems encountered by helpdesk analysts. From application crashes and installation failures to compatibility conflicts and performance slowdowns, users often rely on IT support to resolve software-related challenges. Whether dealing with productivity suites, web browsers, operating systems, or specialized enterprise applications, helpdesk analysts must be equipped with troubleshooting techniques to diagnose and resolve these issues efficiently. Understanding the most commonly used applications, their typical failure points, and best practices for software maintenance is essential for providing effective support.

One of the most widely used software suites in business environments is Microsoft 365 (formerly Office 365), which includes applications such as Word, Excel, PowerPoint, Outlook, and Teams. Users frequently report issues such as crashes, missing features, slow performance, and synchronization errors. Microsoft Outlook, for example, is a common source of support requests due to email synchronization failures, search index corruption, and problems with add-ins. Helpdesk analysts must know how to troubleshoot these issues by repairing the Outlook profile, clearing the cache, rebuilding the search index, or disabling conflicting add-ins. Excel users often report problems with large files causing slow performance, formula errors, or compatibility issues with macros, requiring adjustments to file formats, recalculations, or enabling proper add-ons.

Another major category of software issues involves web browsers such as Google Chrome, Mozilla Firefox, Microsoft Edge, and Safari. Users frequently encounter slow browsing speeds, unresponsive pages, login failures, and website compatibility problems. Common troubleshooting steps include clearing the browser cache, disabling extensions, resetting browser settings, and checking for outdated versions. Some corporate environments enforce group policies that restrict browser settings, leading to user confusion when they cannot modify configurations. Analysts should understand how to manage these restrictions, either through local policy settings or enterprise management consoles.

Operating system-related issues are another significant area of software support. Windows, macOS, and Linux each have their own set of challenges that require specialized troubleshooting techniques. In Windows environments, common problems include failed updates, boot errors, missing drivers, and blue screen errors (BSODs). Helpdesk analysts must be familiar with tools such as Windows Update Troubleshooter, System File Checker (sfc /scannow), and DISM

(Deployment Image Servicing and Management) to repair system corruption. Mac users may experience issues with permissions errors, system performance slowdowns, or software incompatibility after macOS updates, which can often be resolved by resetting NVRAM/PRAM, running Disk Utility, or reinstalling system components. Linux users may face package dependency conflicts, broken repositories, or bootloader failures, requiring the use of command-line tools such as APT, YUM, or GRUB recovery procedures.

Enterprise software, including Customer Relationship Management (CRM) systems like Salesforce, Enterprise Resource Planning (ERP) software like SAP, and collaboration tools like Slack and Zoom, also generate frequent support requests. Users may report login failures, data synchronization errors, missing features, or connectivity issues. Many of these applications rely on cloud-based authentication and integrations with other services, meaning that troubleshooting often involves verifying API connections, clearing authentication tokens, or resetting user permissions. Analysts must also be familiar with server-side troubleshooting, as some issues may be related to backend configurations rather than user-side problems.

Security and antivirus software can also lead to software support issues, especially when they block legitimate applications, interfere with system performance, or prevent network access. Common security suites like Windows Defender, McAfee, Symantec, and Bitdefender may mistakenly identify trusted software as a threat, leading to false positives that require exclusion rules to be configured. Users may also report problems with firewall settings preventing remote access or VPN connections failing to establish due to security restrictions. Helpdesk analysts must balance security enforcement with usability, ensuring that protective measures do not hinder productivity.

Software licensing and activation problems are another frequent source of support requests. Users may encounter errors such as 'Product Key Not Valid' or 'Software Activation Failed' when installing licensed applications. These issues can arise due to expired subscriptions, incorrect license keys, mismatched activation servers, or exceeded device limits. Analysts must understand how to verify activation status, reset licensing configurations, or transfer licenses to new devices. In enterprise environments, software deployment is often managed through tools like Microsoft Endpoint Configuration Manager (SCCM), Jamf, or Intune, which can automate license distribution and compliance enforcement.

One of the most frustrating software issues users experience is application crashes and freezes, which can occur due to corrupted installation files, memory leaks, software conflicts, or insufficient system resources. Diagnosing these problems requires checking event logs, examining error messages, and testing the software in a clean boot environment. Some applications provide built-in diagnostic tools that can generate logs or repair corrupted components automatically. Helpdesk analysts should also be familiar with using Process Explorer or Task Manager (Windows), Activity Monitor (macOS), and system logs (Linux) to identify resource-intensive applications that may be causing system instability.

Software compatibility issues arise when users attempt to run applications that were designed for older operating systems or hardware. Legacy applications may fail to function properly on newer systems due to missing dependencies, deprecated libraries, or unsupported architectures. Solutions for these problems include running the software in compatibility mode, using virtual machines, or utilizing application containerization technologies such as Docker or Windows Sandbox. Some organizations maintain older operating systems specifically for running critical legacy applications that cannot be easily updated.

Patch management is an important aspect of software support, as outdated software versions often lead to compatibility problems and security vulnerabilities. IT teams regularly deploy security patches, feature updates, and bug fixes to ensure applications remain functional and protected against cyber threats. However, software updates can sometimes introduce new issues, leading to performance degradation or broken features. Helpdesk analysts must be able to roll back updates, apply patches selectively, and test software changes in a controlled environment before full deployment.

Helpdesk analysts also play a role in user training and software optimization, helping users understand how to use applications efficiently and avoid common pitfalls. Many software issues arise due to misconfigurations, incorrect usage, or lack of awareness about available features. Providing training sessions, creating documentation, and maintaining a knowledge base of frequently asked questions can reduce the number of support requests and improve overall user proficiency.

Troubleshooting software problems requires a structured approach that includes gathering details about the issue, replicating the problem, checking logs, applying targeted fixes, and verifying the solution with the user. Analysts must stay updated on software trends, new application releases, and emerging security threats to provide the best possible support. A strong foundation in software troubleshooting ensures that IT support teams can resolve issues quickly, minimize downtime, and enhance user productivity across the organization.

Operating Systems: Windows, macOS, and Linux Essentials

Operating systems are the foundation of modern computing, serving as the interface between hardware and software applications. A helpdesk analyst must be familiar with the three major operating systems used in most organizations: Windows, macOS, and Linux. Each of these systems has its own architecture, user interface, and troubleshooting methods, requiring IT support professionals to develop expertise in managing and resolving common issues. Understanding the core functionalities of these operating systems, their file systems, security models, update mechanisms, and system administration tools is essential for providing effective technical support.

Windows is the most widely used operating system in corporate and personal computing environments. Developed by Microsoft, Windows is known for its compatibility with a vast range of applications and hardware configurations. Windows environments often rely on Active Directory (AD) for centralized user authentication and policy management, making it a crucial aspect of enterprise IT support. Helpdesk analysts frequently encounter Windows-related issues such as slow performance, failed updates, driver conflicts, and software crashes. Common troubleshooting steps include using Task Manager to identify resource-intensive processes, Device Manager to check for driver issues, and Event Viewer to analyze system logs. The Command Prompt (cmd) and PowerShell provide additional administrative tools for troubleshooting network issues, managing user accounts, and automating system tasks.

Windows also includes built-in recovery options that help resolve boot failures and critical system errors. The Advanced Startup Options (ASO) menu, accessible via Shift + Restart, provides troubleshooting tools such as System Restore, Startup Repair, Safe Mode, and Command Prompt access. The Windows Update Troubleshooter helps diagnose issues related to failed updates, while the sfc /scannow command scans for and repairs corrupted system files. In enterprise environments, Windows systems are often managed using Group Policy (GPO), Windows Deployment Services (WDS), and Microsoft Endpoint Configuration Manager (SCCM), which allow IT administrators to enforce security policies, deploy updates, and automate software installations.

macOS, the operating system developed by Apple, is widely used in creative industries and business environments that prioritize security and ease of use. Unlike Windows, macOS is built on a UNIX-based architecture, which provides robust system stability and security features. The macOS user interface, known as Finder, simplifies file management, while System Preferences allows users to configure system settings. Helpdesk analysts supporting macOS users frequently deal with Wi-Fi connectivity problems, software installation issues, system slowdowns, and permissions errors. One of the most effective troubleshooting tools for macOS is Disk Utility, which includes First Aid to repair disk errors and verify file system integrity.

Mac computers also include Terminal, a command-line interface similar to Linux's Bash shell, which allows advanced users to execute system commands. The sudo command provides elevated privileges for administrative tasks, while commands like ps aux help monitor system processes. Many common macOS troubleshooting tasks involve resetting the NVRAM/PRAM, which can resolve boot issues, and resetting the System Management Controller (SMC) to fix power and performance problems. Apple's Time Machine provides a built-in backup solution that allows users to restore files or entire system snapshots in case of data loss.

Another key aspect of macOS support is software compatibility. Since macOS restricts software installation to verified applications from the Mac App Store and identified developers, users sometimes experience issues running third-party software. Analysts may need to adjust Security & Privacy settings or use the xattr command to override security restrictions. Additionally, macOS updates are distributed through Software Update in System Preferences, and troubleshooting update failures often involves resetting the NVRAM, deleting cached update files, or reinstalling macOS using macOS Recovery Mode.

Linux is an open-source operating system used in server environments, cybersecurity applications, and development workstations. Unlike Windows and macOS, Linux comes in multiple distributions (distros) such as Ubuntu, CentOS, Fedora, Debian, and Arch Linux. Each distribution has unique package management systems, user interface customizations, and system administration tools. Helpdesk analysts supporting Linux users must be familiar with basic command-line operations, as Linux relies heavily on the Terminal for configuration and troubleshooting.

Linux systems use different package managers depending on the distribution. Debian-based systems like Ubuntu use APT (Advanced Package Tool) for installing and managing software (sudo apt-get install package-name), while Red Hat-based distributions like CentOS use YUM or DNF. Common Linux troubleshooting tasks include checking system logs (journalctl -xe), managing processes (top or htop), and diagnosing network issues (ping, netstat, traceroute). Since Linux provides root access, improper system modifications can lead to critical failures, requiring recovery methods such as chroot environments or booting from a live USB.

File system structures also differ between Windows, macOS, and Linux. Windows primarily uses NTFS (New Technology File System), macOS uses APFS (Apple File System) or HFS+, and Linux supports various file systems such as ext4, XFS, and Btrfs. Understanding file system differences is important when troubleshooting disk permissions, file access errors, and compatibility issues when transferring files between operating systems. Linux and macOS both use POSIX-style file permissions, which involve read, write, and execute attributes for different user levels. The chmod and chown commands allow analysts to modify permissions and ownership for files and directories.

Security models also vary between the three operating systems. Windows implements User Account Control (UAC) to limit administrative privileges, while macOS uses Gatekeeper and SIP (System Integrity Protection) to prevent unauthorized system modifications. Linux follows a least-privilege security model, where users operate in restricted environments unless they explicitly request administrative access using sudo. Many cybersecurity threats exploit weak security configurations, making it crucial for analysts to enforce best practices such as regular updates, strong password policies, and enabling firewalls (Windows Defender, macOS Firewall, or Linux iptables/ufw).

Operating system updates and patch management are critical for maintaining system security and stability. Windows updates are managed through Windows Update, which can be automated via WSUS (Windows Server Update Services) in enterprise environments. macOS updates are deployed through System Preferences > Software Update, and Linux updates are handled via package managers (apt update && apt upgrade for Debian-based systems). When troubleshooting failed updates, analysts often need to clear update caches, manually install patches, or perform rollback procedures.

A helpdesk analyst must also be able to support virtual machines (VMs) and dual-boot environments, as many organizations use virtualization technologies like VMware, VirtualBox, and Hyper-V to run multiple operating systems on a single machine. Common issues include hardware passthrough failures, driver conflicts, and VM network connectivity problems, which require knowledge of hypervisor settings and resource allocation.

Each operating system has unique strengths and challenges, and helpdesk analysts must be proficient in diagnosing and resolving common issues across all three platforms. By mastering Windows, macOS, and Linux troubleshooting techniques, IT professionals can provide comprehensive support to users in diverse computing environments, ensuring smooth system operation and minimizing downtime.

Email Support: Outlook, Gmail, and Exchange

Email is one of the most essential communication tools for businesses and individuals, making email support a crucial responsibility for helpdesk analysts. Whether users rely on Microsoft Outlook, Gmail, or Exchange-based email services, they frequently encounter issues related to login failures, email synchronization, attachment problems, spam filtering, and mailbox management. Effective email troubleshooting requires a strong understanding of email protocols, account configurations, and security settings. Since email-related problems can disrupt productivity, helpdesk analysts must diagnose and resolve them quickly while ensuring compliance with security and organizational policies.

Microsoft Outlook is one of the most widely used email clients, especially in corporate environments that use Microsoft Exchange or Microsoft 365. Users frequently report issues such as slow performance, corrupted profiles, missing emails, and synchronization failures. One of the most common troubleshooting steps involves rebuilding the Outlook profile, which can resolve issues caused by corrupted data files or incorrect settings. This can be done by navigating to the Control Panel > Mail (Microsoft Outlook) > Show Profiles, removing the existing profile, and creating a new one. Additionally, users experiencing slow performance or freezing may need to repair their Outlook data files (.pst and .ost) using the Inbox Repair Tool (scanpst.exe), which helps detect and fix corruption in personal storage files.

Another frequent Outlook issue is email synchronization problems, which can prevent users from receiving or sending messages. This is often caused by network connectivity issues, incorrect server settings, or conflicts with third-party add-ins. Analysts should verify that the Outlook client is connected to the Exchange server by checking the bottom status bar for messages like 'Connected,' 'Disconnected,' or 'Trying to Connect.' If synchronization issues persist, clearing the Outlook cache and resetting the .ost file may resolve the problem. This can be done by navigating to the Outlook account settings, disabling cached exchange mode, deleting the .ost file, and restarting Outlook. If users are experiencing delays in receiving new emails, they may need to adjust the send/receive frequency settings or check whether their mailbox is reaching storage limits.

Outlook users also encounter search-related issues, where they cannot find emails using the search function. This problem is often due to a corrupted search index. To rebuild the search index, analysts should navigate to Control Panel > Indexing Options > Advanced > Rebuild Index. If the issue persists, running sfc /scannow in the Command Prompt may help repair corrupted Windows system files that affect search functionality.

Gmail, Google's cloud-based email platform, is another widely used email service that requires regular support. While Gmail is known for its reliability, users may experience issues such as login failures, email delivery delays, spam filtering problems, and account security concerns. A common issue with Gmail login failures is two-factor authentication (2FA) conflicts, where users are unable to access their accounts due to lost authentication devices. Helpdesk analysts should guide users through the account recovery process, which may involve verifying identity through recovery phone numbers, backup codes, or security questions.

Another Gmail-related issue involves email delivery failures, where users report that sent emails are not reaching recipients or are being marked as spam. Helpdesk analysts should check whether the recipient's email address is correct, verify SPF/DKIM/DMARC records for outgoing email authentication, and review the Gmail outbox for stuck messages. If emails are being flagged as spam, users can adjust Gmail's filter settings, add trusted senders to their contact list, and mark incorrectly labeled emails as 'Not Spam' to improve future email categorization.

Gmail users who access their accounts via third-party email clients such as Outlook or Apple Mail may experience issues due to incorrect IMAP and SMTP settings. Analysts should verify that users have enabled IMAP in their Gmail settings and configured their email client with the correct server details:

IMAP Server: imap.gmail.com (Port 993, SSL required)

SMTP Server: smtp.gmail.com (Port 465 or 587, SSL/TLS required)

If users receive authentication errors when setting up their Gmail accounts in external email clients, enabling 'Allow less secure apps' (for older email clients) or generating an App Password for authentication may be necessary.

Microsoft Exchange is a widely used enterprise email solution that integrates with Active Directory and Outlook for centralized email, calendar, and contact management. Many corporate environments use on-premises Exchange servers or cloud-based Exchange Online (Microsoft 365). Exchange-related issues often involve mailbox access problems, public folder permissions, transport rules, and email flow disruptions. One of the most common Exchange issues is mailbox quota limits, where users are unable to send or receive emails due to exceeding their allocated storage space. Analysts can resolve this by clearing unnecessary emails, archiving older messages, or increasing mailbox limits via Exchange Admin Center (EAC).

Another critical Exchange troubleshooting area is email flow issues, where emails fail to reach recipients. Analysts should check Exchange Transport Logs, Message Tracking Logs, and Queue Viewer to diagnose whether emails are stuck due to blocked connectors, misconfigured transport rules, or SMTP relay failures. Running the Test-Mailflow PowerShell command can help determine if internal email routing is functioning correctly. If emails are being delayed or rejected due to spam filtering, adjusting Exchange's anti-spam policies or whitelisting trusted domains may help resolve the issue.

Exchange users may also experience Outlook Web Access (OWA) login failures, where they are unable to access their email accounts via the web interface. This can be due to expired passwords, incorrect permissions, or IIS (Internet Information Services) configuration errors. Analysts should verify user credentials, reset account passwords if necessary, and check whether Exchange services (IIS, EWS, Autodiscover) are running properly on the Exchange server.

Security plays a significant role in email support, as phishing attacks, malware-infected attachments, and email spoofing pose ongoing threats to businesses. Helpdesk analysts must educate users on how to recognize phishing attempts by checking email headers, verifying sender authenticity, and avoiding clicking on suspicious links. Organizations often implement email filtering solutions, multifactor authentication (MFA), and encryption policies to enhance security. If a user reports a phishing email, analysts should advise them to report the email using built-in phishing reporting tools (Outlook's 'Report Phishing' button, Gmail's 'Report Phishing' option) and update their password if they suspect unauthorized access.

Email troubleshooting also involves mobile device support, as many users access their email accounts through smartphones and tablets. Common mobile email issues include incorrect account settings, sync failures, and push notification problems. Analysts should verify that users have the correct Exchange ActiveSync settings for corporate email accounts and ensure that background data is enabled for email synchronization. Clearing the email app cache, re-adding the email account, or updating the email client can often resolve these issues.

Helpdesk analysts must develop expertise in email troubleshooting to ensure seamless communication within organizations. By understanding the technical aspects of email clients, server configurations, authentication mechanisms, and security measures, analysts can quickly diagnose and resolve email-related problems. Email remains a critical tool for business productivity, making efficient email support an essential skill for IT professionals.

Active Directory: User and Group Management

Active Directory (AD) is a core component of Windows-based enterprise environments, providing centralized management of users, computers, and security policies. IT support professionals, especially helpdesk analysts, frequently interact with Active Directory to manage user accounts, configure security settings, and troubleshoot access-related issues. Understanding how to effectively use Active Directory for user and group management is essential for maintaining a secure and organized IT infrastructure. Helpdesk analysts must be familiar with creating, modifying, disabling, and troubleshooting user accounts, managing group memberships, implementing security policies, and ensuring compliance with organizational access controls.

Active Directory is structured into a hierarchical framework, consisting of domains, organizational units (OUs), groups, and objects. The domain represents the primary boundary for authentication and security policies, while OUs allow administrators to organize resources into logical containers. Within Active Directory, users, groups, and computers are stored as objects that can be managed individually or collectively through Group Policy Objects (GPOs). The Active Directory Users and Computers (ADUC) console is the primary tool used by helpdesk analysts to perform user and group management tasks.

One of the most common tasks in Active Directory management is creating and managing user accounts. New employees require user accounts to be created and configured with the appropriate access levels. Helpdesk analysts typically use the ADUC console to add new users by specifying their username, full name, department, job title, and email address. A strong password policy is enforced to ensure security, often requiring users to create complex passwords with a combination of uppercase and lowercase letters, numbers, and special characters. Some organizations implement password expiration policies, requiring users to change their passwords periodically. If a user forgets their password or is locked out due to multiple failed login attempts, analysts must reset their password and unlock the account through ADUC.

User accounts in Active Directory are often assigned roaming profiles and home directories, allowing users to access their personalized settings from any workstation within the domain. Analysts must ensure that the profile path and home directory permissions are correctly configured to prevent access errors. Misconfigured profile paths can lead to login failures, temporary profile issues, or lost user settings. Additionally, mandatory profiles may be used in environments where users should not be able to make permanent changes to their settings.

Another crucial aspect of Active Directory management is group management, which allows administrators to control access to resources such as shared folders, printers, and applications. Groups in Active Directory are divided into two main types: Security Groups and Distribution Groups. Security Groups are used to manage permissions and access control, while Distribution Groups are used for email distribution lists within Microsoft Exchange.

Security Groups are further classified into Domain Local, Global, and Universal groups, each serving different functions within the Active Directory hierarchy. Domain Local Groups are used to assign permissions to resources within a single domain, while Global Groups are designed for organizing users based on job roles. Universal Groups can span multiple domains within a forest and are typically used in larger enterprise environments. Properly assigning users to the correct groups ensures that they have the necessary permissions to access files, network drives, and applications without granting excessive privileges.

Group membership is often managed through Group Policy Objects (GPOs), which allow administrators to enforce security settings, software installations, and desktop configurations across multiple users. Helpdesk analysts may need to troubleshoot Group Policy issues when users experience unexpected restrictions or lack access to resources. Running the gpupdate /force command or using Group Policy Results (gpresult /r) can help determine whether policies are being applied correctly. If policies fail to propagate, checking Active Directory replication status and reviewing event logs can help identify the cause.

Another important responsibility of helpdesk analysts is disabling and deleting user accounts when employees leave the organization. Disabling accounts prevents unauthorized access while retaining user data for compliance purposes. Many companies follow offboarding procedures that involve disabling the user account, revoking access to shared drives, reassigning email forwarding, and archiving mailbox data. Deleting accounts permanently removes them from Active Directory, but this action should only be taken after verifying that the user's data is no longer needed. Some organizations move deactivated accounts into a separate 'Disabled Users' OU to keep the directory organized while retaining account information.

Password resets are one of the most frequent helpdesk requests in Active Directory environments. Users may be locked out due to forgotten passwords, expired passwords, or multiple failed login attempts. Helpdesk analysts can reset passwords through ADUC or use the PowerShell Set-ADUser -Identity username -ResetPassword command. Many organizations implement self-service password reset (SSPR) portals to reduce the volume of password-related support tickets. Analysts must also educate users on best practices, such as creating secure passwords and enabling multi-factor authentication (MFA) to enhance security.

Active Directory also plays a critical role in Single Sign-On (SSO) and authentication services. Many organizations integrate Azure Active Directory (Azure AD) with on-premises Active Directory to enable cloud-based authentication for applications such as Microsoft 365, Google Workspace, and SaaS platforms. Users experiencing SSO login issues may require a password reset, account re-syncing, or troubleshooting of federation services like AD FS (Active Directory Federation Services).

Helpdesk analysts must also be aware of Active Directory replication and domain controller (DC) health. Replication failures can cause login delays, missing group memberships, or inconsistent policy enforcement across sites. Using tools like repadmin /replsummary and dcdiag helps identify and resolve replication issues. In large organizations with multiple domain controllers, proper replication ensures that user and group changes are synchronized across all domain controllers without delays.

Security within Active Directory is a top priority, as compromised accounts can lead to unauthorized access and data breaches. Analysts should monitor login attempts, account lockouts, and unusual activity using Event Viewer and Security Logs. Enabling Account Lockout Policies helps prevent brute-force attacks, while implementing Least Privilege Access Control ensures that users only have the permissions necessary for their roles.

Automation in Active Directory can improve efficiency in managing user and group accounts. Using PowerShell scripts, IT teams can automate tasks such as bulk user creation, group membership updates, and scheduled password resets. The Active Directory Administrative Center (ADAC) also provides a more user-friendly interface for performing administrative tasks compared to the traditional ADUC console.

Understanding Active Directory user and group management is essential for helpdesk analysts, as it directly impacts security, resource access, and user productivity. By effectively managing user accounts, configuring security groups, and enforcing policies, analysts help maintain a well-organized and secure IT environment. Proper use of Active Directory tools, security best practices, and automation techniques ensures that organizations can efficiently handle user authentication, access control, and directory management while minimizing security risks.

Understanding Permissions and Access Control

Permissions and access control are fundamental concepts in IT security and system administration, ensuring that users have the appropriate level of access to resources while protecting sensitive data. Every operating system, network, and application relies on a structured permissions model to manage how users and groups interact with files, directories, databases, and network resources. Without properly configured access control, organizations risk data breaches, unauthorized modifications, and compliance violations. Helpdesk analysts must understand how permissions work, how they are assigned, and how to troubleshoot access-related issues effectively.

Access control is based on the principle of Least Privilege (PoLP), which means users should only have the permissions necessary to perform their job functions. This minimizes security risks by reducing the chances of accidental data modifications, unauthorized access, or system compromise. Organizations implement access control through Role-Based Access Control (RBAC) and Discretionary Access Control (DAC). RBAC assigns permissions based on predefined job roles, ensuring consistency across similar users. For example, all employees in the finance department may have access to accounting software but not to HR records. In contrast, DAC allows individual users to grant access to resources they own, which can sometimes lead to security vulnerabilities if not managed correctly.

Permissions in Windows environments are primarily managed through NTFS (New Technology File System) permissions and Active Directory (AD) security groups. Every file and folder on an NTFS-formatted drive has an Access Control List (ACL), which contains entries specifying which users and groups can perform actions such as Read, Write, Modify, Execute, and Delete. Administrators can assign permissions at the file level or folder level, and permissions can be inherited from parent directories unless explicitly overridden. If a user reports that they cannot access a file or folder, helpdesk analysts should check the Security tab in the file's Properties menu to review its ACL settings. Running the command icacls filename in Command Prompt provides a detailed breakdown of permissions for a specific file or directory.

In an Active Directory environment, security groups simplify access management by assigning permissions to multiple users at once. Instead of granting permissions individually, users are added to predefined groups such as 'HR Staff' or 'IT Administrators', which inherit appropriate access rights. Analysts frequently troubleshoot issues where users lose access to shared network drives, printers, or applications due to group membership changes. Running whoami /groups in Command Prompt or checking group membership in Active Directory Users and Computers (ADUC) helps determine if a user is part of the correct security groups. If changes do not apply immediately, forcing a Group Policy update using gpupdate /force or verifying Active Directory replication health may be necessary.

Linux and macOS use a POSIX-style permissions model, where every file and directory is associated with an owner, a group, and others. The three main types of permissions are Read (r), Write (w), and Execute (x). These permissions are represented numerically in octal notation, where 777 means full access, 755 allows read and execute permissions but prevents modifications, and 644 allows read access but restricts execution and modifications. The chmod command modifies permissions, while chown and chgrp change file ownership. If a user reports a 'Permission Denied' error while trying to access a file, analysts should check the permissions using ls -l and adjust them accordingly. In some cases, users may need elevated privileges using the sudo command to execute administrative tasks.

Network access control ensures that users can connect to the appropriate network resources while preventing unauthorized access. Permissions for shared folders, mapped network drives, and printers are commonly managed through Shared Folder Permissions and NTFS Permissions in Windows environments. Shared folder permissions dictate access over the network, while NTFS permissions apply locally. If a user cannot access a shared network drive, analysts should check both sets of permissions using Computer Management > Shared Folders and Security tab settings. Running net use in Command Prompt displays active network connections, and gpresult /r helps verify applied policies affecting access.

Databases and cloud applications use role-based access control (RBAC) to restrict data access based on job roles. In database systems like SQL Server, MySQL, and Oracle, permissions are assigned using GRANT and REVOKE commands. A user experiencing database access issues may lack the necessary privileges to query tables, insert records, or execute stored procedures. Analysts should verify user roles and adjust permissions using SQL commands such as GRANT SELECT ON database.table TO username. Cloud platforms such as Google Workspace, Microsoft 365, and AWS IAM (Identity and Access Management) enforce access restrictions using role-based policies, conditional access rules, and multifactor authentication (MFA). An administrator can use Azure Active Directory (AAD) conditional access policies to enforce stricter authentication for sensitive data access.

One of the biggest challenges in access control is permission conflicts and inheritance issues. Users may experience inconsistent access due to overlapping permissions, broken inheritance, or conflicting group policies. For example, if a user is part of multiple groups with different permissions, the most restrictive setting usually takes precedence. Analysts should use tools like Effective Access in Windows or getfacl in Linux to analyze how permissions apply at different levels. If a user unexpectedly loses access, reviewing recent security group modifications, policy updates, or file ownership changes can help pinpoint the cause.

Security concerns in access control include privilege escalation, excessive permissions, and unauthorized access attempts. Cybercriminals often exploit weak access control mechanisms to gain elevated privileges and compromise systems. Analysts should enforce Least Privilege principles, regularly audit group memberships, and review log files for suspicious access attempts. Windows Event Viewer logs audit failures and unauthorized login attempts, while Linux stores access logs in /var/log/auth.log. Implementing account lockout policies, multi-factor authentication (MFA), and access reviews minimizes the risk of unauthorized access.

Automation improves access management efficiency by reducing manual permission assignments. Organizations use Identity and Access Management (IAM) systems like Okta, Azure AD, and SailPoint to automate user provisioning and deprovisioning. Analysts should understand how automated workflows assign roles based on HR records or department attributes, ensuring that employees receive access only to the resources they need. If an automated system fails, verifying synchronization logs, reviewing role mappings, and manually correcting discrepancies can help restore access.

Understanding permissions and access control is crucial for IT support professionals. Whether managing file permissions, Active Directory groups, or cloud-based roles, analysts must ensure that users have the appropriate access while maintaining security. By mastering tools like NTFS permissions, Linux file ownership, role-based access control, and security auditing, analysts can effectively troubleshoot access issues, prevent security breaches, and ensure compliance with organizational policies.

VPN and Remote Access Troubleshooting

Virtual Private Networks (VPNs) and remote access technologies are essential for businesses and individuals who need secure connections to private networks from external locations. With the rise of remote work and cloud computing, VPNs provide encrypted communication between users and corporate resources, ensuring confidentiality and security. However, VPN connections can encounter a range of issues, including authentication failures, slow performance, dropped connections, and compatibility problems. Helpdesk analysts must be equipped with the knowledge and troubleshooting skills necessary to diagnose and resolve these problems efficiently, ensuring users can securely access the resources they need without disruption.

A VPN works by establishing an encrypted tunnel between the user's device and the organization's network, preventing unauthorized access and data interception. Common VPN protocols include OpenVPN, IPSec, L2TP, PPTP, and SSL/TLS-based VPNs. Many enterprises use Cisco AnyConnect, Palo Alto GlobalProtect, Fortinet FortiClient, and OpenVPN for secure remote connectivity. Each VPN type has specific configurations and security policies that must be properly implemented for successful connections. When users experience VPN connectivity issues, the first step is to determine whether the problem is related to client-side settings, network configuration, authentication, or VPN server availability.

One of the most common VPN issues is authentication failure, where users are unable to log in due to incorrect credentials, expired passwords, or misconfigured authentication policies. VPN authentication is often integrated with Active Directory (AD), RADIUS servers, or multifactor authentication (MFA). If a user reports authentication issues, helpdesk analysts should verify their credentials, check for expired passwords, and confirm that their account is not locked out in Active Directory. Additionally, if MFA is enabled, users may need to re-register their authentication devices or check for expired tokens. Analysts can also review RADIUS logs and VPN server authentication logs to identify failed login attempts and diagnose authentication-related errors.

Network-related issues can also cause VPN failures. A user's home or office network may have firewall rules or router settings that block VPN connections. Many VPNs use specific ports for communication, such as UDP 1194 for OpenVPN, TCP 443 for SSL VPNs, and UDP 500/4500 for IPSec-based VPNs. If these ports are blocked by the user's firewall or ISP, the VPN connection may fail to establish. Helpdesk analysts should instruct users to temporarily disable firewalls or antivirus software to determine if they are interfering with the VPN connection. Running network diagnostic commands such as ping, tracert, and nslookup can help identify whether the user's device can reach the VPN server.

Another frequent VPN issue is IP conflict and DNS resolution failure, where users can connect to the VPN but cannot access internal resources such as file shares, databases, or internal web applications. This is often due to incorrect DNS settings, split tunneling misconfigurations, or overlapping subnets between the user's home network and the corporate network. Analysts should check whether the VPN client is assigning the correct internal IP address by running ipconfig /all (Windows) or ifconfig (Linux/macOS). If DNS resolution is failing, manually setting the corporate DNS servers in the VPN client configuration or flushing the DNS cache using ipconfig /flushdns can resolve the issue. Additionally, editing the hosts file or using nslookup to test name resolution can help diagnose DNS-related VPN failures.

Performance issues, such as slow VPN speeds, high latency, and frequent disconnections, are common complaints among remote users. These problems may be caused by congested network routes, server-side bandwidth limitations, or encryption overhead. VPN traffic is often encrypted using AES-256 or SSL/TLS protocols, which require processing power that can slow down performance on older devices. If users experience laggy VPN connections, analysts should check their internet speed using tools like Speedtest.net and advise them to switch to a wired Ethernet connection instead of Wi-Fi. Some VPN clients allow users to select different VPN gateways or lower encryption levels to improve performance. If the VPN server is experiencing high loads, users may benefit from connecting to an alternative server or switching between TCP and UDP protocols for better stability.

VPN clients can also be affected by software conflicts, outdated versions, or corrupted installations. If a VPN application is failing to launch or crashes frequently, reinstalling the VPN client or updating to the latest version can resolve compatibility issues. Many VPN providers release patches and firmware updates to fix known bugs and security vulnerabilities. If users receive error messages such as 'Unable to establish a VPN session' or 'Connection reset by peer', reviewing the VPN logs located in the application's installation directory can provide insights into the cause of the failure. Additionally, running the VPN client as an administrator or in compatibility mode may help resolve permission-related issues.

Security policies can also prevent successful VPN connections. Many organizations enforce Zero Trust Network Access (ZTNA) policies, conditional access rules, and network segmentation to limit VPN access based on user roles and device compliance. If a user is unable to access specific corporate resources after connecting to the VPN, their device may not meet security requirements such as up-to-date antivirus protection, OS patches, or device posture compliance. Helpdesk analysts should check the VPN policy logs and verify whether the user's device has the necessary certificates, endpoint protection software, or security group assignments required for access.

Some enterprises utilize Always-On VPN and split tunneling configurations, which affect how traffic is routed through the VPN tunnel. Always-On VPN forces all traffic through the corporate network, enhancing security but sometimes causing performance degradation. Split tunneling allows internet traffic to bypass the VPN, improving speed but potentially exposing users to security risks. If users report that external websites or cloud applications are inaccessible while connected to the VPN, checking the split tunneling settings in the VPN client configuration is necessary. Enabling or disabling split tunneling based on company policies can help resolve network routing issues.

Mobile devices also experience VPN-related challenges, particularly when using IPSec or SSL VPNs on Android and iOS devices. Users may report that their VPN disconnects frequently when switching between Wi-Fi and cellular networks. Mobile VPNs often require per-app VPN settings, persistent VPN connections, or specific APN configurations to maintain connectivity. Ensuring that the VPN app has the necessary permissions to run in the background, allowing data usage in low-power mode, and disabling battery optimizations can help maintain a stable connection.

Helpdesk analysts must also be prepared to escalate VPN issues to network administrators when necessary. If multiple users report VPN failures, the issue may be related to VPN server downtime, expired SSL certificates, incorrect NAT configurations, or firewall rule misconfigurations on the corporate network. Running netstat -an on the VPN server, checking IKE and IPsec logs, and monitoring VPN gateway performance metrics can help diagnose infrastructure-related issues.

Troubleshooting VPN and remote access issues requires a structured approach that includes verifying authentication settings, checking network connectivity, diagnosing performance bottlenecks, and ensuring compliance with security policies. By understanding the technical intricacies of VPN protocols, network configurations, and encryption methods, helpdesk analysts can provide efficient support to remote users, ensuring seamless and secure access to corporate resources from any location.

Mobile Device Support: iOS and Android Basics

Mobile devices have become essential tools for both personal and professional use, and IT support teams are frequently tasked with troubleshooting issues related to iOS and Android devices. Whether users are experiencing connectivity issues, software glitches, app crashes, or security concerns, helpdesk analysts must be well-versed in the fundamentals of both operating systems to provide efficient support. As businesses increasingly rely on mobile devices for email, collaboration, and remote access, understanding mobile device management (MDM), security settings, and common troubleshooting techniques is crucial for maintaining productivity and security.

Understanding iOS and Android Operating Systems

iOS, developed by Apple, is a closed ecosystem that prioritizes security and stability. It is used exclusively on Apple devices such as the iPhone and iPad. Apple enforces strict App Store policies, meaning apps must be verified before installation. iOS updates are managed centrally, ensuring that most users are running the latest software versions. However, troubleshooting iOS devices can be challenging due to the limited customization options and lack of user-level system access.

Android, developed by Google, is an open-source operating system used by a wide range of manufacturers, including Samsung, Google, OnePlus, and Motorola. Unlike iOS, Android allows for extensive customization, including third-party app installations and alternative ROMs. This flexibility makes troubleshooting more complex, as device settings and user interfaces can vary significantly between manufacturers. Android updates are also fragmented, meaning that different devices may run different versions of the operating system, leading to inconsistencies in support.

Common Mobile Connectivity Issues

One of the most frequent problems reported by mobile users is network connectivity issues, which may involve Wi-Fi, mobile data, or Bluetooth failures. If a user cannot connect to Wi-Fi, helpdesk analysts should instruct them to toggle Airplane Mode on and off, forget and reconnect to the Wi-Fi network, reset network settings, or reboot the device. On iOS, network settings can be reset by navigating to Settings > General > Reset > Reset Network Settings, while on Android, users can go to Settings > System > Reset options > Reset Wi-Fi, mobile & Bluetooth.

Cellular data issues may arise due to incorrect APN settings, SIM card malfunctions, or carrier outages. Analysts should verify that mobile data is enabled, check for carrier updates, and confirm that the user is in an area with network coverage. If mobile data is not working after a software update, checking for a carrier settings update or manually configuring APN settings may resolve the issue.

Bluetooth issues often occur when devices fail to pair or maintain a stable connection. Users should be advised to remove and re-pair Bluetooth devices, reset network settings, and ensure that Bluetooth accessories are charged and in pairing mode. On Android, clearing the Bluetooth cache via Settings > Apps > Show System Apps > Bluetooth > Storage > Clear Cache can sometimes resolve persistent pairing issues.

Email and Application Troubleshooting

Business users frequently rely on mobile devices for email access, making email synchronization problems one of the most common support requests. iOS users accessing corporate email through Microsoft Exchange or Outlook should check that their accounts are correctly configured under Settings > Mail > Accounts and that background app refresh is enabled. If emails fail to sync, removing and re-adding the email account or checking for iOS software updates may resolve the problem.

Android users accessing corporate email through Gmail or Microsoft Outlook should verify their sync settings, enable auto-sync in Settings > Accounts > Google, and check whether battery optimization settings are interfering with background processes. Many Android devices have aggressive power-saving modes that restrict email synchronization. If emails are delayed, whitelisting the email app in Battery Optimization settings can help maintain consistent synchronization.

Application-related issues on both iOS and Android may include app crashes, freezes, or login failures. Troubleshooting steps typically include force-closing the app, clearing the cache (Android), checking for updates, and reinstalling the application. On iOS, reinstalling an app requires deleting it from the home screen and downloading it again from the App Store. On Android, users can clear the app cache and data through Settings > Apps > [App Name] > Storage > Clear Cache & Clear Data before attempting a reinstall.

Security and Device Management

Security is a primary concern for mobile device support, especially when dealing with corporate devices that contain sensitive information. Many organizations use Mobile Device Management (MDM) solutions such as Microsoft Intune, VMware Workspace ONE, or Google's Android Enterprise to enforce security policies, remote wipe lost devices, and restrict access to corporate applications. If a user is unable to install a company-approved app or access corporate resources, analysts should check whether their device is enrolled in the correct MDM profile and that all required security policies are applied.

Users often report issues related to device encryption, biometric authentication, or passcode policies. iOS devices require Face ID, Touch ID, or passcodes for security enforcement, while Android devices may use PINs, patterns, or fingerprint authentication. If a user forgets their passcode on iOS, they will need to erase the device via iCloud's Find My iPhone or restore it using iTunes/Finder. On Android, failed unlock attempts may require a Google account recovery or, in some cases, a factory reset if the device is permanently locked.

Phishing and malware threats are increasing on mobile platforms, particularly through malicious links sent via SMS (smishing) or compromised apps. Analysts should educate users on how to recognize phishing attempts, avoid downloading apps from untrusted sources, and report suspicious activity to IT security teams. Many enterprises enforce device compliance policies, ensuring that employees install security updates, enable device encryption, and avoid rooting or jailbreaking their devices.

Battery and Performance Issues

Users frequently report battery drain and slow performance as common mobile complaints. On iOS, checking battery health under Settings > Battery > Battery Health & Charging can indicate whether a device needs servicing. If battery drain is excessive, disabling background app refresh, reducing screen brightness, and turning off location services for unnecessary apps can help extend battery life.

On Android, many manufacturers include battery optimization settings that limit background activity. If an app is not functioning properly due to restricted background processes, whitelisting it in Settings > Battery > Battery Optimization can improve performance. Slow performance on older devices can often be attributed to low storage space, excessive background processes, or outdated software. Advising users to clear cached data, uninstall unused apps, and update their OS can help maintain optimal device performance.

Providing support for iOS and Android devices requires a combination of technical knowledge, troubleshooting skills, and an understanding of enterprise security policies. Helpdesk analysts must be prepared to assist users with connectivity issues, email synchronization problems, app crashes, security configurations, and device management policies. By mastering these fundamentals, IT support teams can ensure that users remain productive and secure while using their mobile devices for both work and personal use.

Cloud Computing: Microsoft 365, Google Workspace, and SaaS Applications

Cloud computing has revolutionized the way organizations manage their IT infrastructure, offering scalable, flexible, and cost-effective solutions for productivity, collaboration, and data storage. Services such as Microsoft 365, Google Workspace, and other Software-as-a-Service (SaaS) applications allow businesses to reduce their reliance on on-premises hardware while enabling employees to access essential tools from anywhere. Helpdesk analysts must understand how these cloud-based platforms operate, how they authenticate users, and how to troubleshoot common issues related to connectivity, permissions, data synchronization, and security settings.

Microsoft 365 is one of the most widely used cloud productivity suites, integrating applications such as Outlook, Teams, OneDrive, SharePoint, Word, Excel, and PowerPoint into a single ecosystem. Users rely on Exchange Online for email, OneDrive for Business for personal file storage, and SharePoint Online for collaborative document management. Authentication in Microsoft 365 is typically managed through Azure Active Directory (Azure AD), which supports single sign-on (SSO), multi-factor authentication (MFA), and conditional access policies to enforce security requirements.

One of the most common Microsoft 365 issues users experience is login failures, which may occur due to incorrect passwords, expired credentials, or account lockouts. Helpdesk analysts should first verify whether the user can log into the Microsoft 365 portal (https://office.com) using their credentials. If the account is locked or the password has expired, resetting the password through Azure AD or the Microsoft 365 Admin Center is the next step. If MFA is enabled, users may need to update their authentication methods, such as switching to a different MFA device or generating an app password for legacy applications.

Another frequent issue in Microsoft 365 involves email synchronization failures in Outlook. Users may report missing emails, delayed deliveries, or problems accessing shared mailboxes. Analysts should first check whether the user is using cached Exchange mode, which can sometimes cause synchronization delays. Clearing the Outlook cache, recreating the mail profile, or running the Microsoft Support and Recovery Assistant (SaRA) tool can resolve most email-related problems. If a shared mailbox is not appearing, verifying the permissions in Exchange Online and ensuring that the user is a member of the correct security group is essential.

Microsoft Teams is another critical component of Microsoft 365, facilitating real-time collaboration through chat, video conferencing, and file sharing. Common problems include Teams not loading, messages failing to send, or microphone and camera issues. Analysts should check for Teams service outages in the Microsoft 365 Service Health dashboard, clear the Teams cache, and ensure that the correct audio and video devices are selected in the application's settings. If Teams does not sync properly with OneDrive or SharePoint, resetting the OneDrive sync client and re-authenticating in Teams may help resolve the issue.

Google Workspace, formerly known as G Suite, provides cloud-based productivity tools such as Gmail, Google Drive, Google Docs, Google Sheets, and Google Meet. Unlike Microsoft 365, which integrates with on-premises Active Directory environments, Google Workspace relies on Google Accounts and Google Admin Console for user management and authentication. Helpdesk analysts supporting Google Workspace users frequently encounter login issues, file access permissions problems, and email delivery failures.

When a user is unable to log into their Google Workspace account, analysts should first verify whether the Google Admin Console (https://admin.google.com) shows any account restrictions. If the account is suspended, verifying the reason for the suspension—such as multiple failed login attempts or security policy violations—is necessary. If the user has forgotten their password, a password reset can be initiated through the admin console. Users with MFA enabled may need to generate backup codes or reconfigure their authentication apps to regain access.

Gmail issues commonly involve email delivery delays, missing emails, or spam filtering errors. Helpdesk analysts should check the Gmail Message Header for delivery timestamps and analyze the Email Log Search feature in the Google Admin Console to determine whether an email was blocked or routed incorrectly. If emails are not syncing in third-party email clients like Outlook or Apple Mail, verifying IMAP and SMTP settings, clearing the email cache, and ensuring that 'Allow less secure apps' is enabled (if required) can help resolve the issue.

Google Drive is a major component of Google Workspace, allowing users to store, share, and collaborate on files in the cloud. Users may experience problems such as sync failures, permission errors, or file version conflicts. Analysts should check whether Google Drive File Stream (now Google Drive for Desktop) is installed and running properly. If sync failures occur, users can be instructed to restart the sync client, clear the Google Drive cache, or manually re-upload files. If a user cannot access a shared file, verifying whether the document owner has granted the correct permissions is essential.

SaaS applications extend beyond Microsoft 365 and Google Workspace, covering a broad range of business tools such as Salesforce, Dropbox, Slack, Zoom, and Asana. These applications are hosted in the cloud and typically require browser-based authentication or SSO integration with identity providers like Azure AD or Okta. Users often encounter issues such as failed logins, missing data, slow performance, or integration failures with other services.

Browser-related problems are common with SaaS applications, particularly when users experience login loops, blank pages, or session timeouts. Clearing browser cookies and cache, disabling problematic extensions, and ensuring that the browser is up to date can often resolve these issues. If an application relies on pop-ups for authentication, ensuring that pop-up blockers are disabled for trusted domains is necessary. Additionally, if a SaaS platform fails to integrate with another cloud service, checking API connection settings and reauthorizing the integration may be required.

Security concerns in cloud computing involve data loss prevention, unauthorized access, and compliance with corporate policies. Many organizations implement Data Loss Prevention (DLP) policies, access control lists (ACLs), and conditional access rules to safeguard sensitive information. Helpdesk analysts may need to troubleshoot access restrictions, policy violations, or account suspensions due to security rules. Ensuring that users are enrolled in the correct groups, have the necessary permissions, and follow security best practices is critical for maintaining a secure cloud environment.

Managing cloud-based applications requires familiarity with user provisioning, licensing models, storage quotas, and data migration tools. Both Microsoft 365 and Google Workspace provide administrative dashboards that allow IT teams to monitor system health, allocate licenses, and track usage analytics. If users exceed their OneDrive or Google Drive storage limits, they may need to delete files, purchase additional storage, or transfer files to shared storage solutions like SharePoint or Google Shared Drives.

As cloud computing continues to evolve, helpdesk analysts must stay updated on new features, security policies, and troubleshooting techniques for Microsoft 365, Google Workspace, and SaaS applications. Understanding the intricacies of cloud platforms allows IT support teams to assist users effectively, resolve technical challenges, and ensure seamless access to business-critical applications from any location.

Security Awareness and Best Practices for Helpdesk Analysts

Security is one of the most critical aspects of IT support, and helpdesk analysts play a vital role in ensuring that users follow security best practices while protecting organizational assets from cyber threats. Since helpdesk analysts often serve as the first line of defense against phishing attacks, data breaches, malware infections, and unauthorized access, they must be well-versed in security protocols, policies, and risk mitigation strategies. A strong understanding of security awareness not only helps protect sensitive information but also reinforces a culture of cybersecurity within the organization.

One of the primary security concerns for helpdesk analysts is user authentication and identity management. Weak passwords, repeated password reuse, and credential leaks are among the most common security vulnerabilities. To mitigate these risks, organizations enforce strong password policies requiring a combination of uppercase and lowercase letters, numbers, and special characters. Helpdesk analysts must encourage users to create unique passwords for each account and enable multi-factor authentication (MFA) whenever possible. MFA adds an extra layer of security by requiring users to verify their identity through a secondary authentication method, such as a one-time passcode (OTP), authentication app, or biometric verification.

Social engineering attacks, including phishing, vishing (voice phishing), and smishing (SMS phishing), remain significant threats to organizations. Cybercriminals frequently attempt to trick employees into revealing login credentials, financial information, or confidential data by posing as trusted individuals or organizations. Helpdesk analysts must be trained to recognize common phishing tactics, such as urgent requests for sensitive information, fake login pages, and email attachments containing malware. If a user reports a suspicious email, the analyst should advise them not to click on any links or download any attachments and forward the email to the organization's security team for further investigation. Analysts should also educate users on verifying sender addresses, checking for spelling errors in fraudulent emails, and hovering over links to inspect their true destinations before clicking.

Another key security responsibility of helpdesk analysts is secure account management. When users request password resets or access changes, analysts must verify their identities through established security procedures. Granting access to unauthorized individuals can lead to data breaches and compliance violations. Analysts should follow strict verification processes, such as confirming user identity through predefined security questions, manager approvals, or identity verification via corporate authentication systems. Additionally, analysts should log all account changes and escalations to ensure accountability and track potential security incidents.

Remote access security is another critical aspect of helpdesk operations. Many employees work remotely, requiring access to corporate resources through Virtual Private Networks (VPNs), remote desktop connections, or cloud-based applications. Ensuring that users connect securely by using encrypted VPNs, secure Wi-Fi networks, and company-approved remote access tools minimizes the risk of unauthorized access. If a user reports connectivity issues, analysts should ensure that they are using up-to-date VPN clients, following corporate security policies, and not connecting through unsecured public Wi-Fi networks. If remote sessions are required, analysts should use tools that enforce multi-factor authentication, session timeouts, and encrypted connections to protect against session hijacking or unauthorized access.

Workstation security is also an essential component of security best practices. Analysts should enforce automatic screen locks, restricted USB device usage, and endpoint protection measures to prevent unauthorized access to company systems. If a user reports that their device has been lost or stolen, the helpdesk must act immediately by remotely locking the device, wiping sensitive data, and revoking access to corporate accounts. Many organizations implement Mobile Device

Management (MDM) solutions to manage and secure employee devices, ensuring compliance with security policies even when devices are outside the corporate network.

Software and system updates play a crucial role in preventing security vulnerabilities. Cybercriminals often exploit outdated software to gain unauthorized access to systems through unpatched vulnerabilities. Helpdesk analysts must ensure that users regularly update their operating systems, browsers, antivirus software, and enterprise applications to the latest security patches. Many organizations use automated patch management systems to enforce timely updates, reducing the risk of exploits targeting outdated software. If a user reports issues after a system update, analysts should troubleshoot compatibility issues while ensuring that critical security updates are not disabled or ignored.

Handling sensitive data responsibly is a fundamental principle of security awareness. Helpdesk analysts must understand data classification policies, ensuring that confidential information is only accessible to authorized individuals. Analysts should never store or transmit user credentials, personally identifiable information (PII), or financial data in unencrypted emails or unsecured locations. Organizations often enforce Data Loss Prevention (DLP) policies to detect and prevent unauthorized data transfers, blocking attempts to share sensitive files outside approved channels. If a user reports difficulty accessing protected data, analysts should verify role-based access permissions and audit logs to ensure that security policies are correctly enforced.

Incident response and reporting procedures are crucial for mitigating security threats effectively. If a security incident occurs, such as unauthorized access, malware infection, or data leakage, helpdesk analysts must follow predefined incident response protocols to contain and escalate the issue. This includes gathering relevant logs, isolating affected systems, notifying security teams, and assisting in forensic investigations. Proper documentation of security incidents helps organizations analyze trends, improve security policies, and prevent future breaches.

Security training and awareness programs help reinforce cybersecurity best practices across the organization. Helpdesk analysts play an active role in educating users on secure behaviors, such as recognizing phishing attempts, reporting suspicious activity, and safeguarding corporate assets. Conducting security awareness sessions, sending out cybersecurity bulletins, and promoting secure password management tools can help reduce human errors that lead to security breaches.

Compliance with industry standards and regulations is another responsibility of IT support teams. Many organizations must adhere to security frameworks such as GDPR, HIPAA, ISO 27001, and NIST cybersecurity guidelines. Helpdesk analysts must understand the basic principles of data protection, regulatory compliance, and access control policies to ensure that security measures align with industry best practices. If users require access to sensitive systems, analysts should verify that they meet compliance requirements before granting permissions.

By implementing security best practices, helpdesk analysts contribute significantly to an organization's overall security posture. Their vigilance in monitoring security threats, enforcing access controls, educating users, and following proper incident response procedures ensures that corporate systems remain protected from evolving cyber threats. A strong culture of security awareness among IT support professionals helps mitigate risks, prevent unauthorized access, and safeguard organizational data against potential breaches.

Phishing and Social Engineering Attacks: How to Spot and Prevent Them

Phishing and social engineering attacks are among the most prevalent cybersecurity threats faced by organizations and individuals today. Cybercriminals use these tactics to manipulate users into revealing sensitive information, such as login credentials, financial data, or company secrets. Unlike traditional cyberattacks that rely on exploiting technical vulnerabilities, phishing and social engineering target human psychology, making them particularly dangerous.

Helpdesk analysts play a crucial role in identifying, mitigating, and educating users about these threats. Understanding how these attacks work, recognizing their warning signs, and implementing preventive measures are essential for maintaining security and preventing unauthorized access to sensitive information.

Phishing attacks typically occur through fraudulent emails, fake websites, or malicious links designed to trick users into providing personal information. These emails often impersonate trusted entities, such as banks, government agencies, or well-known companies. Attackers use urgent language, fake login pages, or enticing offers to lure victims into clicking on malicious links or downloading malware-infected attachments. One of the most common forms of phishing is credential harvesting, where attackers create a counterfeit website resembling a legitimate service, prompting users to enter their login credentials. Once credentials are entered, they are captured by the attacker and used for unauthorized access.

One of the key indicators of a phishing email is inconsistencies in the sender's email address. Attackers often use spoofed email addresses that appear similar to legitimate domains but contain slight misspellings or extra characters. For example, an email claiming to be from support@paypal.com might instead come from support@paypall.com or admin@paypal-secure.com. Users should always verify the sender's domain before responding to emails requesting sensitive information. Hovering over email links without clicking them can reveal the actual destination URL, helping users detect fraudulent websites before they fall victim to an attack.

Another common phishing tactic involves urgent or alarming messages designed to create a sense of panic. Attackers may claim that a user's account has been compromised, a payment has failed, or legal action is pending unless immediate action is taken. These emails often contain phrases like 'Your account will be locked in 24 hours' or 'Verify your identity now to prevent suspension.' This urgency pressures users into acting without carefully inspecting the email. Helpdesk analysts should train users to recognize these tactics and advise them to independently verify such claims by contacting the company directly using official contact information rather than clicking on links provided in the email.

Another variation of phishing is spear phishing, a targeted attack aimed at specific individuals within an organization. Unlike generic phishing emails, spear phishing emails are carefully crafted using personalized details, such as the recipient's name, job title, or recent activity, to appear more convincing. Attackers may conduct research on social media platforms like LinkedIn to gather information about their targets. A spear phishing email might impersonate an executive or IT support representative, requesting a password reset or financial transaction approval. Helpdesk analysts should encourage users to verify unexpected requests for sensitive actions through an independent communication channel, such as a direct phone call or internal messaging platform.

Whaling is a specialized form of spear phishing that targets high-ranking executives, such as CEOs, CFOs, or directors. These attacks often involve fraudulent requests for wire transfers, financial transactions, or confidential company data. Because whaling emails appear to come from senior management, employees may feel pressured to comply without questioning the legitimacy of the request. Organizations should implement strict approval workflows and multi-factor authentication (MFA) for financial transactions to prevent unauthorized fund transfers resulting from social engineering attacks.

Another prevalent social engineering attack is vishing (voice phishing), where attackers use phone calls to impersonate legitimate entities. In these attacks, cybercriminals may pose as IT support, bank representatives, or government officials to extract sensitive information from unsuspecting individuals. A common tactic involves calling a user and claiming their computer has been infected with malware, instructing them to install remote access software to 'fix the issue.' Once installed, the attacker gains control over the system, allowing them to steal credentials, install additional malware, or demand ransom payments. Helpdesk analysts should educate users on the dangers of unsolicited phone calls requesting sensitive information and encourage them to verify callers before providing any data.

Smishing (SMS phishing) is another form of social engineering that exploits text messages to trick users into clicking malicious links or providing personal information. Attackers send SMS messages that appear to come from banks, delivery services, or government agencies, containing messages such as 'Your package is delayed. Click here to update your delivery information.' If the recipient clicks the link, they may be directed to a fake website designed to capture login credentials or financial details. Users should be advised to avoid clicking on links from unknown senders and instead visit official websites directly by typing the URL into their browser.

To mitigate the risks associated with phishing and social engineering, organizations should implement security awareness training programs that teach employees how to recognize and report suspicious activity. Regular phishing simulation tests can help employees become more vigilant in identifying fraudulent emails. Organizations should also enforce email filtering solutions to block known phishing domains and prevent malicious attachments from reaching users' inboxes.

Multi-factor authentication (MFA) is one of the most effective defenses against phishing attacks. Even if an attacker successfully steals a user's password, they will be unable to access the account without the second authentication factor, such as a time-based one-time passcode (TOTP) or biometric verification. Helpdesk analysts should ensure that MFA is enabled on all critical accounts and educate users on the importance of securing their authentication methods.

Another important security measure is domain-based message authentication, reporting, and conformance (DMARC), sender policy framework (SPF), and domain keys identified mail (DKIM), which help authenticate emails and prevent attackers from spoofing legitimate domains. Organizations should configure these security protocols to reduce the likelihood of phishing emails impersonating internal employees.

Helpdesk analysts should also encourage users to report phishing attempts to the IT security team for further analysis. Many email platforms, including Microsoft Outlook and Gmail, offer built-in options to report phishing emails directly. IT teams can use reported phishing data to update email filtering rules, block malicious domains, and enhance security awareness training.

By understanding how phishing and social engineering attacks work, helpdesk analysts can proactively protect users, enforce security best practices, and reduce the risk of cyber threats within the organization. These attacks continue to evolve, requiring constant vigilance and adaptation of security strategies to keep users and company data safe.

Common Error Messages and How to Resolve Them

Error messages are a common part of IT support, often serving as the first clue in diagnosing and resolving technical issues. Helpdesk analysts frequently encounter a wide range of error messages related to operating systems, applications, network connectivity, and hardware failures. Understanding what these messages mean and how to troubleshoot them efficiently is essential for providing timely and effective support. While some errors have straightforward fixes, others require deeper investigation to identify the root cause and implement a solution.

One of the most frequent errors in Windows operating systems is 'Blue Screen of Death (BSOD)', which occurs when a critical system error forces Windows to shut down to prevent damage. BSOD errors typically include a STOP code that provides insight into the cause of the failure. Common BSOD errors include 'CRITICAL_PROCESS_DIED,' 'MEMORY_MANAGEMENT,' 'PAGE_FAULT_IN_NONPAGED_AREA,' and 'DRIVER_IRQL_NOT_LESS_OR_EQUAL.' To troubleshoot these errors, analysts should check for recent hardware or driver changes, run Windows Memory Diagnostic to test RAM, and update or roll back drivers. Using Event Viewer and analyzing the minidump files can also provide additional clues about the underlying problem.

Another common Windows error message is 'Windows Cannot Find [filename]. Make Sure You Typed the Name Correctly.' This typically occurs when a file or application shortcut is missing, moved, or corrupted. Users should check whether the file exists in its expected location, ensure the correct file path is being used, and scan for system file corruption using sfc /scannow in Command Prompt. If the error is related to an application, reinstalling the program can often restore missing components.

For macOS users, one of the most frequently encountered errors is 'The application 'App Name' is not open anymore.' This issue typically occurs when an application crashes or becomes unresponsive. The first step in resolving this problem is to force quit the application using Command + Option + Esc, then relaunch it. If the error persists, users should check Activity Monitor to see if any background processes are causing conflicts. Clearing app preferences in the Library folder, reinstalling the application, or updating macOS to the latest version can also help resolve persistent crashes.

Network-related errors are another frequent issue that helpdesk analysts must address. One of the most common errors in both Windows and macOS is 'No Internet, Secured' or 'Connected but No Internet Access.' This error indicates that the device is connected to a Wi-Fi network but cannot reach external websites. Troubleshooting steps include resetting the network adapter using ipconfig /release and ipconfig /renew, rebooting the router, and flushing the DNS cache using ipconfig /flushdns. If the issue persists, checking whether a firewall or VPN is blocking internet access can help diagnose the root cause.

Users frequently report email errors when trying to send or receive messages in Outlook, Gmail, or other mail clients. One common error in Outlook is 'ox800ccc0e: Cannot Connect to the Server.' This error occurs when the email client cannot establish a connection with the mail server. Helpdesk analysts should verify SMTP and IMAP/POP3 settings, check for firewall or antivirus interference, and ensure the mail server is not experiencing downtime. If using Microsoft 365, running the Microsoft Support and Recovery Assistant (SaRA) tool can help diagnose and automatically fix email synchronization problems.

Login-related errors are among the most frustrating issues for users, particularly in enterprise environments. One common Active Directory login error is 'The Trust Relationship Between This Workstation and the Primary Domain Failed.' This occurs when the computer account in Active Directory becomes out of sync with the domain controller. To resolve this, analysts should remove the computer from the domain, restart the device, and rejoin it to the domain. Running the command netdom resetpwd /server:domaincontroller /userd:domain\admin /passwordd:* can also help reset the machine's trust relationship without removing it from the domain.

Software installation errors are another frequent problem, particularly on Windows systems. A common error when installing or updating software is 'Error 1603: A Fatal Error Occurred During Installation.' This error usually indicates a conflict with an existing application or permission issues. Analysts should check whether the software is already installed, run the installer as an administrator, disable conflicting background applications, and ensure that system permissions allow installation in the target directory.

For users working with Microsoft Teams, a common issue is 'We're Sorry – We've Run Into an Issue' when attempting to sign in. This problem is often caused by corrupt cache files. Clearing the Teams cache by deleting the contents of %appdata%\Microsoft\Teams and restarting the application typically resolves the problem. If the issue persists, reinstalling Teams or checking for service outages in the Microsoft 365 Admin Center may be necessary.

Printer-related errors are also common helpdesk issues. One of the most frustrating printer errors in Windows is 'Printer is Offline,' even when the printer is powered on and connected. This error can often be resolved by checking the printer's status in the 'Devices and Printers' section of the Control Panel, restarting the print spooler service using net stop spooler and net start spooler, and ensuring the printer is set as the default device. If printing issues persist, reinstalling the printer drivers or updating firmware may be required.

For Windows Update failures, a common error message is 'Windows Update Failed to Install' with error codes like 0x80070002 or 0x80240034. These errors can occur due to corrupt update files, insufficient disk space, or conflicts with existing software. Running the Windows Update Troubleshooter, clearing the SoftwareDistribution folder, and manually downloading updates from the Microsoft Update Catalog are effective troubleshooting steps.

Web browser errors are another frequent support issue, especially with Google Chrome, Microsoft Edge, and Mozilla Firefox. One of the most common browser errors is 'ERR_CONNECTION_TIMED_OUT,' which occurs when the browser cannot establish a connection to the requested website. Troubleshooting this issue involves clearing the browser cache, disabling browser extensions, resetting network settings, and ensuring that the website is not blocked by a firewall or proxy server.

Cloud storage services such as OneDrive, Google Drive, and Dropbox also generate frequent errors related to sync failures and access permissions. A common OneDrive error is 'Files are not syncing' or 'OneDrive is not connected.' This issue can often be resolved by signing out and back into the OneDrive client, checking for storage space limits, and ensuring that the sync folder is correctly configured.

Understanding and resolving common error messages is a fundamental skill for helpdesk analysts. Whether dealing with operating system errors, software failures, network connectivity problems, or email issues, knowing the right troubleshooting steps can significantly reduce downtime and improve user experience. Proper documentation of error resolutions also helps build a knowledge base, making it easier to resolve recurring issues efficiently.

Printer and Peripheral Troubleshooting

Printers and peripherals such as keyboards, mice, scanners, and external drives are essential components of modern computing environments, but they are also frequent sources of frustration for users. Helpdesk analysts often receive tickets related to printer connection failures, print quality issues, unresponsive peripherals, and driver conflicts. Troubleshooting these devices effectively requires a structured approach, starting with basic checks and progressing to more advanced diagnostics. Understanding the common causes of printer and peripheral malfunctions allows analysts to quickly restore functionality and minimize disruptions to users.

One of the most common printer issues reported to IT support is 'Printer is Offline,' even when the device is powered on and connected to the network. This problem is often caused by communication failures between the computer and the printer. The first step in troubleshooting is to verify the printer's connection type—whether it is connected via USB, Wi-Fi, or Ethernet. If the printer is connected via USB, trying a different cable or port can help rule out hardware failures. If the printer is networked, pinging the printer's IP address can determine if it is reachable. If the printer does not respond, checking network configurations, restarting the router, or assigning a static IP address to the printer may be necessary.

Another frequent printing issue is print jobs getting stuck in the queue. Users often report that they send documents to the printer, but nothing happens. This is usually due to a problem with the Print Spooler service, which manages print jobs in Windows. Restarting the print spooler using the commands net stop spooler and net start spooler in Command Prompt often resolves the issue. If the print queue remains stuck, manually deleting queued jobs from the C:\Windows\System32\spool\PRINTERS folder can clear any corrupted files preventing printing.

Users also encounter problems where print quality is poor, with documents appearing faded, smudged, or containing missing sections. If a printer produces faded or incomplete prints, checking the toner or ink levels should be the first step. In laser printers, replacing a low or leaking toner cartridge and cleaning the drum unit can improve print quality. In inkjet printers, clogged printheads are a common cause of quality issues. Running the printer's built-in cleaning cycle and manually cleaning the printhead with a lint-free cloth and distilled water can help restore proper function.

Another common issue is paper jams, where users report that paper is stuck inside the printer. Paper jams typically occur due to misaligned paper trays, using the wrong paper size, or worn-out rollers. When resolving a paper jam, instruct users to remove paper carefully without tearing it, check for any remaining fragments, and ensure that the paper tray is properly adjusted. If jams occur frequently, cleaning the feed rollers with isopropyl alcohol and ensuring that users are using the correct type of paper for the printer model can help prevent recurrence.

Network printers may also experience intermittent connectivity issues, where the printer goes offline sporadically. This can be caused by DHCP lease expirations, weak Wi-Fi signals, or firewall restrictions. Assigning a static IP address to the printer prevents network disconnections. For Wi-Fi printers, ensuring that the device is within range of the wireless router and checking for firmware updates can improve stability. If a printer is part of a Windows print server environment, verifying the server status and group policy settings is necessary to ensure that shared printers are correctly mapped to client devices.

Besides printers, helpdesk analysts frequently troubleshoot peripheral devices such as keyboards, mice, and external storage devices. A common issue with USB keyboards and mice is that they suddenly stop responding. This can be caused by driver conflicts, faulty USB ports, or power management settings. Plugging the device into a different USB port and testing it on another computer helps determine if the issue is with the peripheral itself or the computer's USB ports. In Windows, checking Device Manager for errors related to the keyboard or mouse driver and reinstalling drivers often resolves connectivity problems. If a wireless keyboard or mouse stops functioning, replacing the batteries and re-pairing the device with its receiver should be attempted before further troubleshooting.

External storage devices, such as USB flash drives and external hard drives, sometimes fail to appear when connected to a computer. If a user reports that their device is not being recognized, the first step is to check Disk Management in Windows (diskmgmt.msc) or Disk Utility on macOS to see if the drive is detected but not assigned a letter. If the drive appears but is unallocated or has a RAW file system, formatting may be necessary to restore functionality. If an external drive is completely unrecognized, testing it on another computer and trying a different USB cable can help determine if the issue is with the drive or the host system.

Scanners also generate frequent support requests, particularly in offices that rely on multi-function printers (MFPs). A common error users face is 'Scanner Not Found' or 'Cannot Communicate with the Scanner.' This often results from outdated drivers, firewall settings blocking the connection, or incorrect scanning software settings. Ensuring that the scanner is properly installed in Device Manager (Windows) or System Preferences (macOS), reinstalling drivers, and verifying that scanning software such as Windows Fax and Scan, Adobe Acrobat, or proprietary scanner utilities is configured correctly can help resolve these issues.

Webcams and microphones, especially in remote work environments, are other peripherals that often require troubleshooting. If a webcam is not detected, checking Privacy Settings in Windows (Settings > Privacy & Security > Camera) to ensure that apps have permission to use the camera is essential. For microphone issues, verifying that the correct input device is selected in Sound Settings and ensuring that it is not muted are the first steps. Updating drivers, checking for conflicting applications, and running the Windows Troubleshooter for audio and video devices can resolve most webcam and microphone-related problems.

Docking stations and USB hubs can also create issues where connected devices do not work properly. Some docking stations require additional power adapters to function correctly, and using an underpowered hub can cause devices to disconnect randomly. Ensuring that users are using manufacturer-recommended accessories, updating docking station firmware, and checking for BIOS updates on laptops can improve compatibility.

Troubleshooting printers and peripherals requires a systematic approach that includes checking power and connections, verifying drivers, testing alternative ports, and diagnosing potential software conflicts. Many issues can be resolved through basic maintenance, driver updates, or firmware patches, while more complex problems may require hardware replacements or network configuration changes. Helpdesk analysts must be prepared to resolve a wide range of issues efficiently, ensuring that users can work without disruptions caused by faulty printers and peripherals.

Voice and Telephony Support: VoIP and PBX Basics

Voice and telephony support is a crucial function of IT helpdesk teams, ensuring that users can communicate effectively within and outside the organization. Traditional telephony systems have evolved significantly, with most businesses now relying on Voice over Internet Protocol (VoIP) or Private Branch Exchange (PBX) systems for voice communication. Understanding how these systems work, troubleshooting common telephony issues, and managing configurations effectively is essential for providing seamless voice communication support.

VoIP technology allows users to make voice calls over the internet rather than through traditional phone lines. Unlike analog telephone systems that rely on circuit-switched networks, VoIP converts voice signals into digital packets and transmits them using IP (Internet Protocol). This provides greater flexibility, cost savings, and integration with other IT systems. Popular VoIP solutions include Cisco Unified Communications, Microsoft Teams Phone, Avaya, Asterisk, 3CX, and Zoom Phone. Businesses use VoIP to enable internal office communication, call routing, voicemail-to-email services, and remote work connectivity.

One of the most common VoIP issues reported to IT support teams is call quality degradation, which can manifest as choppy audio, dropped calls, one-way audio, or delays (latency and jitter). These problems are often related to network congestion, insufficient bandwidth, misconfigured Quality of Service (QoS) settings, or problems with the VoIP provider. Helpdesk analysts should first check the user's network conditions by running a speed test to measure download/upload speeds and packet loss. If the network has high latency or jitter, adjusting QoS settings on the router to prioritize VoIP traffic can improve call stability. Additionally, verifying that the user's firewall is not blocking SIP (Session Initiation Protocol) traffic and ensuring that the correct ports (such as UDP 5060 for SIP signaling and UDP 10000-20000 for RTP audio streams) are open can help resolve connectivity issues.

Another frequent issue in VoIP systems is users being unable to make or receive calls. If a user reports that their VoIP phone is unresponsive or not registering, the first step is to verify whether the VoIP service is operational by checking the phone system's status in the administration portal. Ensuring that the user's device has a valid IP address, the VoIP client is properly configured, and SIP credentials are correctly entered is also important. If an IP-based VoIP phone is not functioning, power cycling the device, testing with a different network cable, or resetting to factory settings can help restore connectivity.

Some users may experience one-way audio issues, where they can hear the caller but are not heard, or vice versa. This is often caused by NAT (Network Address Translation) issues, incorrect port forwarding, or firewall restrictions. Ensuring that NAT traversal settings are configured correctly on the VoIP server and enabling SIP ALG (Application Layer Gateway) in the router settings can help resolve these issues. If using a cloud-hosted VoIP system, confirming that the correct STUN (Session Traversal Utilities for NAT) or TURN (Traversal Using Relays around NAT) servers are specified in the VoIP client settings can improve audio transmission reliability.

Voicemail configuration and management are another important aspect of VoIP and PBX support. Users often request help with voicemail setup, voicemail-to-email integration, and message retrieval issues. In most VoIP systems, voicemail settings are managed through an administrative dashboard where IT teams can reset PINs, assign voicemail boxes, and configure automatic voicemail transcription services. If users report that voicemails are not being delivered to their email, verifying email server integration settings and checking for spam filtering rules that may be blocking the messages is essential.

PBX (Private Branch Exchange) systems are used by many businesses to manage internal and external phone calls. Traditional PBX systems relied on physical hardware and analog lines, but modern implementations use IP-PBX systems, which integrate with VoIP and provide advanced call routing, auto-attendants, and conference calling capabilities. Common PBX platforms include Asterisk, FreePBX, Elastix, and Avaya IP Office.

One of the most common PBX-related issues is incorrect call routing, where incoming calls are not reaching the intended recipient or are being misrouted to the wrong extension. This can occur due to misconfigured call flow settings, incorrect extension mappings, or automatic call forwarding rules. Helpdesk analysts should verify the PBX dial plan and call routing rules in the administrative interface to ensure that calls are being directed correctly. If call forwarding is enabled unintentionally, disabling it via *feature codes (such as 73 for call forwarding deactivation in some PBX systems) or through the PBX portal can resolve the issue.

Users also report issues related to conference calls and call drops, particularly when using softphones or mobile VoIP applications. If users are unable to join conference calls, confirming that they have the correct dial-in numbers and access PINs is the first step. Ensuring that the PBX system allows multiple concurrent calls per extension and that SIP trunk limits are not exceeded can prevent dropped conference calls. If a VoIP client fails to maintain a stable connection during long calls, adjusting keep-alive settings and SIP session timers can help maintain consistent connectivity.

Security is a major concern in VoIP and PBX environments. Unauthorized access, toll fraud (where attackers make unauthorized international calls), and SIP-based attacks pose risks to businesses. IT teams should enforce strong SIP authentication credentials, implement access control lists (ACLs) to restrict VoIP access to known IP addresses, and enable encryption protocols such as TLS for SIP signaling and SRTP (Secure Real-Time Transport Protocol) for voice transmission. If unusual activity is detected, such as high call volumes to international numbers or repeated failed login attempts on SIP trunks, reviewing VoIP logs and blocking suspicious IP addresses is necessary.

Many organizations also use softphones—software-based VoIP applications that allow users to make and receive calls using their computers or mobile devices instead of physical desk phones. Common softphone applications include Cisco Jabber, Zoiper, Bria, and Microsoft Teams Phone. Users frequently encounter issues such as audio not working, microphone permissions being blocked, or poor call quality. Ensuring that the softphone application has the necessary permissions to access the microphone and speakers, updating audio drivers, and verifying that the correct audio devices are selected in the settings can resolve most issues.

VoIP and PBX troubleshooting requires a combination of networking knowledge, system configuration skills, and an understanding of telephony protocols. By systematically diagnosing issues related to call quality, connectivity, routing, voicemail, and security, helpdesk analysts can ensure that users experience seamless voice communication, reducing downtime and improving overall productivity.

Scripting and Automation for Helpdesk Analysts

Scripting and automation are becoming essential skills for helpdesk analysts, enabling them to streamline repetitive tasks, improve efficiency, and reduce human errors in IT support processes. By leveraging scripting languages such as PowerShell, Bash, Python, and batch scripting, analysts can automate various aspects of troubleshooting, account management, software deployment, and system monitoring. As IT environments grow increasingly complex, the ability to create and implement automation tools enhances a helpdesk analyst's productivity and allows IT teams to focus on more critical support issues.

One of the most common uses of scripting in a helpdesk environment is automating user account management tasks in Active Directory (AD). Helpdesk analysts frequently perform tasks such as creating new user accounts, resetting passwords, modifying group memberships, and disabling accounts for offboarding employees. Instead of manually executing these actions through the Active Directory Users and Computers (ADUC) console, analysts can use PowerShell scripts to simplify and speed up the process. For example, a PowerShell script to bulk-create user accounts from a CSV file might include commands such as New-ADUser to automatically generate accounts with predefined attributes. Similarly, a script using Set-ADUser can automate password resets and Disable-ADAccount can quickly deactivate former employees' accounts.

Another valuable area of automation is system monitoring and diagnostics. Helpdesk analysts frequently investigate issues related to CPU usage, memory consumption, disk space, and network connectivity. Instead of manually checking these metrics on multiple machines, they can use scripting to gather and report system health data. A PowerShell script utilizing Get-Process, Get-WmiObject Win32_LogicalDisk, and Test-Connection can generate real-time system health reports for troubleshooting performance issues. Bash scripts can achieve similar results in Linux environments, using commands such as top, df -h, and ping to monitor resource usage and network connectivity.

Software installation and patch management are other areas where scripting can significantly reduce manual effort. Instead of installing applications one by one on multiple machines, analysts can use automated deployment scripts. PowerShell, for instance, can be used to install applications silently using Windows Package Manager (winget) or Chocolatey, while Bash scripts can be used to automate package installations with APT or YUM on Linux systems. Automating software deployment ensures consistency across multiple devices and reduces the risk of missing critical updates.

One of the most common scripting applications in IT support is automating ticket management in helpdesk systems. Many IT teams use ticketing systems such as ServiceNow, Zendesk, or Jira, which have APIs that allow for automation. Analysts can write scripts that automatically categorize, assign, and update tickets based on predefined conditions. A Python script utilizing the ServiceNow API, for example, can extract unresolved tickets, escalate high-priority issues, and send automated follow-ups to users. By integrating scripting with helpdesk workflows, analysts can reduce manual data entry and improve response times.

Another frequent request in IT support is gathering system logs for troubleshooting. Instead of manually navigating through event logs, analysts can use PowerShell to filter and extract relevant logs using Get-EventLog or Get-WinEvent. For Linux systems, a Bash script using journalctl -xe or tail -n 100 /var/log/syslog can quickly display recent system errors. Automating log retrieval allows analysts to diagnose recurring issues more efficiently and standardizes troubleshooting procedures.

In addition to troubleshooting, scripting can be used to enhance security by automating compliance checks and enforcing security policies. PowerShell can be used to scan for inactive user accounts, failed login attempts, and unauthorized administrator access using Search-ADAccount and Get-EventLog -LogName Security. Analysts can also automate scheduled security audits, ensuring that critical security policies such as password expiration, MFA enforcement, and group membership reviews are consistently applied.

Network troubleshooting is another area where scripting proves useful. Instead of manually running ipconfig /all, tracert, or nslookup on multiple devices, analysts can automate network diagnostics using PowerShell or Python. A PowerShell script that checks network adapter status, default gateway, and DNS settings can be executed remotely to identify connectivity issues without requiring manual intervention. Python scripts can integrate with tools like Scapy and Nmap to automate network scans and detect open ports, latency issues, and misconfigured firewalls.

One often overlooked but valuable use of automation is email and notification management. Helpdesk analysts frequently send repetitive email responses related to password resets, system outages, or scheduled maintenance. Using PowerShell's Send-MailMessage or Python's smtplib, analysts can automate email notifications to users, reducing the time spent on routine communications. Automated scripts can also be configured to send alerts for critical system failures, ensuring that IT teams are informed of potential problems before they escalate.

For teams managing cloud services such as Microsoft 365 and Google Workspace, automation plays a crucial role in account provisioning, license management, and compliance monitoring. PowerShell scripts using Microsoft Graph API can automate the creation of Microsoft 365 users, assignment of licenses, and reporting of security compliance metrics. Similarly, Google Admin SDK can be integrated with Python scripts to manage Google Workspace users, enforce security policies, and retrieve audit logs.

Virtual machine (VM) and server maintenance tasks can also be automated to improve efficiency. IT teams managing VMware, Hyper-V, or cloud-based instances in AWS, Azure, or Google Cloud can use scripts to automate snapshot creation, reboot VMs on a schedule, and deploy updates without manual intervention. PowerShell modules such as Az for Azure, AWS CLI for AWS, and gcloud for Google Cloud allow analysts to interact with cloud environments programmatically, reducing the time required for routine maintenance.

Helpdesk teams handling large-scale user support requests can also benefit from automation in chatbots and self-service tools. By integrating scripts with Slack, Microsoft Teams, or chat-based IT support platforms, organizations can create automated chatbots that assist users with common troubleshooting tasks, password resets, and knowledge base lookups. Python scripts leveraging Natural Language Processing (NLP) models can enhance chatbot responses, making them more effective in assisting users with IT-related inquiries.

For ongoing maintenance and process optimization, helpdesk teams can use automation to generate IT performance reports, tracking average resolution times, most common support requests, and system health metrics. Python scripts using pandas and matplotlib can analyze helpdesk data, identifying trends that help IT teams optimize workflows and reduce repeat issues.

Mastering scripting and automation empowers helpdesk analysts to improve efficiency, reduce human errors, and focus on high-priority IT support tasks. Whether automating Active Directory management, software deployment, system monitoring, or helpdesk ticketing workflows, analysts who develop scripting skills gain a competitive advantage in IT support roles. Investing in PowerShell, Bash, Python, and API integrations significantly enhances productivity, allowing IT teams to deliver faster, more consistent, and proactive support services.

Performance Monitoring and Basic System Diagnostics

Performance monitoring and system diagnostics are essential tasks for helpdesk analysts, as they enable IT teams to identify and resolve issues related to slow system performance, high CPU and memory usage, disk failures, network slowdowns, and software crashes. By using built-in system tools and diagnostic utilities, analysts can detect performance bottlenecks, troubleshoot hardware or software failures, and ensure that systems operate efficiently. Understanding how to monitor system resources and interpret diagnostic results is crucial for maintaining productivity and preventing downtime.

One of the most common complaints from users is slow system performance, which can be caused by excessive CPU usage, insufficient RAM, high disk activity, or background processes consuming system resources. In Windows environments, Task Manager is the primary tool for monitoring real-time performance metrics. Analysts can open Task Manager using Ctrl + Shift + Esc and check the Processes tab to identify applications consuming excessive CPU or memory. If a process is using an abnormally high percentage of resources, force-closing it and investigating its cause can help restore system performance. The Performance tab provides an overview of CPU, memory, disk, and network usage, allowing analysts to detect resource constraints.

For macOS users, Activity Monitor serves the same purpose as Task Manager, providing insights into CPU, memory, energy, disk, and network usage. If an application is unresponsive or consuming excessive resources, force-quitting it from Activity Monitor can help regain system stability. Analysts should also check the Memory Pressure graph to determine if a system is running low on available RAM, which can lead to slow performance due to excessive swapping between RAM and the disk.

Another critical aspect of system diagnostics is disk health monitoring, as failing hard drives or solid-state drives (SSDs) can cause data loss and system instability. In Windows, the chkdsk (Check Disk) command allows analysts to scan for file system errors and bad sectors. Running chkdsk /f /r from an elevated Command Prompt checks the disk for corruption and attempts to repair damaged sectors. Additionally, the S.M.A.R.T. (Self-Monitoring, Analysis, and Reporting Technology) status of a drive can be checked using the wmic diskdrive get status command or third-party tools like CrystalDiskInfo. If a drive is reporting a S.M.A.R.T. failure, immediate data backup and replacement of the disk are necessary.

In macOS, Disk Utility provides a graphical interface for checking and repairing disk errors. Running First Aid on a drive allows the system to scan for file system inconsistencies and fix minor corruption issues. If a Mac system fails to boot due to disk corruption, booting into macOS Recovery Mode (Cmd + R at startup) and using Disk Utility to repair the drive can often resolve startup failures.

Helpdesk analysts must also monitor RAM usage and potential memory leaks, as insufficient memory can cause frequent application crashes and sluggish performance. In Windows, the resmon (Resource Monitor) tool provides a more detailed view of memory allocation, showing which processes are consuming the most RAM. If a system is frequently running out of memory, increasing the virtual memory (page file) size through Advanced System Settings or upgrading physical RAM may be necessary. In Linux, memory usage can be monitored using the free -m command, while the vmstat tool provides real-time memory and CPU usage statistics.

Network diagnostics are another crucial area of system performance monitoring, as slow internet speeds, dropped connections, and high latency can impact business operations. Analysts often start troubleshooting by using the ping command to check connectivity between the user's device and a remote server. If packet loss or high latency is detected, further analysis using tracert (Windows) or traceroute (Linux/macOS) can reveal where the connection is slowing down. Running ipconfig /all (Windows) or ifconfig (Linux/macOS) provides details about network adapters, IP addresses, and DNS settings, helping analysts determine if an incorrect configuration is causing connectivity issues.

For users experiencing Wi-Fi performance problems, verifying the signal strength and interference levels is critical. Many routers operate on the 2.4 GHz and 5 GHz frequency bands, and congestion on the 2.4

GHz band can cause slow speeds. Using tools like Wi-Fi Analyzer or the built-in netsh wlan show networks mode=bssid command in Windows helps identify which channels are being used by surrounding networks. Reconfiguring the router to use a less congested channel can improve connectivity.

Application crashes and system instability can often be diagnosed by analyzing system logs and error messages. In Windows, the Event Viewer (eventvwr.msc) provides detailed logs on system errors, application crashes, and hardware failures. Analysts should check the System and Application logs for recurring error messages and use the associated event ID to find potential solutions. For example, Event ID 41 (Kernel-Power) indicates an unexpected shutdown, which may be due to hardware failure, overheating, or power supply issues. In Linux, log files stored in /var/log/syslog or /var/log/dmesg provide similar insights into system activity and failures.

Another useful diagnostic tool in Windows is Performance Monitor (perfmon), which allows analysts to create detailed performance reports on CPU, memory, disk, and network activity. Configuring Data Collector Sets enables IT teams to log system performance over time and identify trends that may indicate an impending hardware failure. Mac users can achieve similar functionality using Console.app, which provides access to system logs and crash reports.

Thermal management is another aspect of system diagnostics, as overheating can cause performance degradation, automatic shutdowns, and hardware damage. Using tools such as HWMonitor (Windows), iStat Menus (macOS), or lm-sensors (Linux) allows analysts to monitor CPU and GPU temperatures in real time. If temperatures exceed safe operating limits, ensuring proper ventilation, cleaning dust from cooling fans, and replacing thermal paste can help lower temperatures.

Automated system health checks can further enhance performance monitoring. PowerShell scripts such as Get-Process for CPU usage, Get-WmiObject Win32_LogicalDisk for disk health, and Test-NetConnection for network diagnostics can be scheduled to run at regular intervals, alerting IT teams to potential issues before they escalate. In Linux environments, cron jobs can be used to automate log analysis, disk space monitoring, and service status checks.

Preventive maintenance also plays a role in system diagnostics. Regularly updating software, drivers, and firmware ensures that security patches and performance improvements are applied. Checking for Windows Update failures using wuauclt /detectnow and running sudo apt update && sudo apt upgrade in Linux helps keep systems secure and stable. Additionally, ensuring that antivirus software is up to date and scanning regularly prevents malware-related performance degradation.

By mastering performance monitoring and system diagnostics, helpdesk analysts can efficiently identify the root causes of slow performance, hardware failures, software crashes, and network issues. Using built-in system tools, analyzing logs, and leveraging automation improves troubleshooting speed and ensures that users experience minimal disruptions. Having a structured approach to diagnostics helps IT teams maintain reliable and high-performing computing environments across organizations.

Documentation and Knowledge Base Management

Effective documentation and a well-organized knowledge base are the cornerstones of efficient IT support and long-term organizational success. Helpdesk analysts, system administrators, and IT teams rely on comprehensive, accurate, and easily accessible documentation to resolve issues swiftly, train new staff, and maintain consistency across various processes. The process of capturing solutions, system configurations, troubleshooting procedures, and best practices ensures that valuable information is not lost when employees leave or when technology evolves. Creating, maintaining, and continuously updating a knowledge base empowers IT professionals to resolve recurring issues, reduce resolution times, and improve user satisfaction by providing clear guidance and reliable reference materials.

One of the fundamental aspects of documentation management is the initial creation of thorough and clear records. Every time a helpdesk analyst encounters a problem and finds a solution, it is essential to document the process in detail. This documentation should include the symptoms reported by the user, the diagnostic steps taken, any troubleshooting scripts or tools used, and the final resolution. By documenting these processes, IT teams build a repository of insights that can serve as a first line of defense for similar issues in the future. This repository not only reduces the need for repeated troubleshooting but also aids in identifying trends that might indicate systemic problems within the IT environment. Accurate documentation allows teams to develop standard operating procedures that can be refined over time as new technologies emerge and user needs evolve.

A robust knowledge base management system goes beyond simple documentation; it integrates various tools and platforms to ensure that information is organized, searchable, and easily retrievable. Modern knowledge base systems offer features such as tagging, categorization, and search functionalities that allow helpdesk analysts to quickly locate the right information when time is of the essence. Whether the information is stored in an internal wiki, a dedicated knowledge management system, or even in a shared document repository, the key is to ensure that it is structured in a way that makes sense to both experienced IT professionals and those who are new to the field. Well-organized documentation supports collaborative efforts and encourages knowledge sharing among team members, fostering an environment where continuous learning is valued.

The importance of keeping documentation up to date cannot be overstated. Technology is constantly evolving, and processes that worked well a few months ago may no longer be applicable. As updates are rolled out, systems are reconfigured, or new software is deployed, the documentation must be reviewed and revised accordingly. This requires a disciplined approach where regular audits of the knowledge base are conducted to remove outdated information and incorporate new insights. Assigning ownership for documentation ensures that specific team members are responsible for maintaining sections of the knowledge base and that there is accountability for the accuracy and relevance of the content. In environments where documentation is treated as a living resource, IT teams experience a significant reduction in troubleshooting time and improved overall efficiency.

Moreover, creating documentation that is both comprehensive and understandable is a critical skill for helpdesk analysts. Technical language should be used judiciously, with an emphasis on clarity and simplicity. When a solution is documented, it should be written in a manner that allows non-technical users, as well as new team members, to grasp the essential steps without confusion. Including examples, screenshots, and diagrams can enhance understanding and reduce the likelihood of misinterpretation. Effective documentation also aids in training and onboarding processes, as it provides a consistent reference that can be used to instruct new employees and help them quickly get up to speed on common issues and solutions.

Integrating user feedback into the documentation process further strengthens the knowledge base. Helpdesk analysts often interact with end users and gain valuable insights into what information is most helpful when resolving issues. Encouraging users to provide feedback on documented solutions can highlight areas that may need additional detail or clarification. This iterative process of refinement helps build a more robust and user-friendly resource that benefits both the IT team and the wider organization. As more issues are resolved and added to the knowledge base, the collective experience of the support team grows, allowing for a more proactive approach to common problems.

The use of modern collaboration tools has transformed knowledge base management. Platforms such as Confluence, SharePoint, and even collaborative tools like Microsoft Teams or Slack allow team members to contribute to documentation in real time. These tools often include version control, so any changes made to documents are tracked, and previous versions can be restored if necessary. This ensures that the knowledge base remains consistent and that the evolution of troubleshooting techniques is recorded over time. Collaboration also promotes a sense of shared responsibility, where each team member can contribute insights, leading to a more comprehensive repository of knowledge that benefits the entire organization.

Another important aspect of documentation management is establishing standard formats and templates. When every piece of documentation follows a consistent structure, it becomes much easier for team members to locate the information they need quickly. Standard templates for troubleshooting guides, system configuration documents, and user manuals ensure that critical details are not omitted and that the documentation maintains a professional standard. This consistency not only aids in the efficiency of problem resolution but also creates a more organized and credible knowledge base that can be trusted by both internal stakeholders and external auditors.

In addition to technical documentation, creating detailed reports on system performance, user issues, and recurring errors can be a valuable resource for long-term planning. By analyzing trends within the knowledge base, IT managers can identify recurring problems and take proactive steps to address underlying issues. This data-driven approach to support not only improves system reliability but also contributes to strategic decision-making regarding IT infrastructure investments and process improvements.

Ensuring that the knowledge base is accessible to all relevant team members is essential for maximizing its benefits. Access controls should be implemented so that the documentation remains secure yet available to those who need it. Integrating the knowledge base with the ticketing system allows helpdesk analysts to reference solutions directly within the support workflow, reducing the time required to resolve issues. Making documentation available through mobile devices or cloud-based platforms ensures that support staff can access critical information even when they are away from their desks.

Effective documentation and knowledge base management create an environment where IT support becomes more proactive and efficient. By capturing and organizing the collective knowledge of the IT team, organizations can respond more quickly to issues, reduce redundancy in troubleshooting efforts, and continuously improve their support processes. A well-maintained knowledge base serves as a valuable asset that not only aids in day-to-day operations but also contributes to long-term strategic planning and the overall success of the organization.

Service Level Agreements (SLAs) and Why They Matter

Service Level Agreements (SLAs) are essential contracts between a service provider and its customers that define the expected level of service, performance metrics, and responsibilities. In IT support and helpdesk environments, SLAs establish clear expectations for response times, resolution times, and service availability, ensuring that both users and IT teams understand their roles and commitments. By implementing well-structured SLAs, organizations improve accountability, enhance customer satisfaction, and maintain efficiency in IT service delivery.

SLAs typically outline key performance indicators (KPIs) that measure the effectiveness of IT support operations. These KPIs include first response time, resolution time, uptime percentage, and escalation procedures. First response time refers to how quickly a helpdesk analyst acknowledges a support request, while resolution time defines the timeframe within which the issue must be resolved. Uptime percentage measures the availability of critical systems, ensuring that users experience minimal downtime. Escalation procedures specify the steps to be taken if an issue cannot be resolved within the agreed timeframe, including the involvement of higher-level support teams or management.

Different types of SLAs exist depending on the nature of the service and the organization's requirements. A customer-based SLA applies to a single customer or department, specifying the level of service tailored to their needs. For example, an enterprise IT team might provide a higher priority response time to executives compared to standard employees. A service-based SLA applies to a specific service, such as email support, where all users receive the same level of service regardless of their position. A multi-level SLA is a more complex structure that defines different levels of service for various user groups, internal teams, or service providers, ensuring that IT support aligns with business priorities.

One of the most critical aspects of SLAs is defining prioritization levels based on the urgency and impact of an issue. Not all support requests are equal; a network outage affecting an entire department requires a much faster resolution than a minor software installation request. Most IT organizations use a priority matrix that categorizes issues into different levels: Critical (P1), High (P2), Medium (P3), and Low (P4). Critical issues, such as server failures or security breaches, require immediate attention and must be resolved within hours, while low-priority issues, such as cosmetic software bugs, may have a resolution time of several days.

Enforcing SLAs requires the use of a ticketing system that tracks incidents, response times, and resolution progress. Systems like ServiceNow, Zendesk, Jira Service Management, and Freshdesk automatically log support requests, assign priority levels, and send reminders when SLA deadlines are approaching. If an issue is not resolved within the defined SLA timeframe, the system can trigger escalation workflows, notifying senior analysts or managers to ensure that the issue receives the necessary attention.

IT support teams must communicate SLAs clearly to end users, as misunderstandings about response and resolution times can lead to frustration. When users submit a support request, they should receive an automated response confirming their ticket's priority level, estimated resolution time, and next steps. Providing users with access to a self-service knowledge base can also help reduce ticket volume by allowing them to resolve minor issues independently.

SLAs play a crucial role in vendor and third-party service management. Many IT services rely on external providers, such as cloud service vendors, internet service providers (ISPs), and managed IT services. These providers also operate under SLAs that define expected uptime, support response times, and compensation for service failures. If a cloud provider guarantees 99.9% uptime, any deviation from this commitment may entitle the organization to service credits or other compensation. IT teams must monitor vendor SLAs to ensure that third-party services meet organizational requirements and escalate issues if the provider fails to deliver as promised.

SLAs also contribute to continuous service improvement (CSI) by providing measurable performance data. IT managers analyze SLA compliance reports to identify recurring issues, measure technician efficiency, and adjust workflows. If a service desk consistently fails to meet SLA targets for a particular issue type, it may indicate a need for additional training, process adjustments, or resource allocation. Regular SLA reviews ensure that service commitments align with changing business needs and technological advancements.

One challenge in SLA management is balancing efficiency with realistic expectations. Setting unrealistically short resolution times can lead to burnout among IT staff and reduced service quality. On the other hand, overly generous SLAs may result in poor user experience and delayed issue resolution. Organizations must strike a balance that allows IT teams to resolve issues efficiently without compromising quality. Regular discussions between IT leaders, service providers, and business stakeholders help refine SLAs to meet both technical and business objectives.

A well-structured SLA includes clear definitions of service scope, exclusions, and limitations. It is important to define what the IT team is responsible for and what falls outside the scope of their support. For example, an SLA may specify that the helpdesk provides support for company-issued laptops but not for personal devices unless explicitly authorized. Setting clear boundaries prevents unnecessary workload and ensures that users understand which services are covered and which are not.

SLAs also play a role in disaster recovery and business continuity planning. In the event of a major system failure, cybersecurity incident, or natural disaster, organizations must have emergency response SLAs to ensure that critical services are restored as quickly as possible. High-priority services such as email servers, cloud storage, and communication platforms may have aggressive SLA targets, ensuring that they are prioritized in recovery efforts.

Security and compliance are also factors in SLA design. Many industries, such as healthcare, finance, and government, require IT services to adhere to strict security and privacy regulations. SLAs may include data protection commitments, access control policies, and incident response timeframes to ensure compliance with standards such as GDPR, HIPAA, and ISO 27001. Ensuring that security policies are integrated into SLAs protects both the organization and its users from potential data breaches and regulatory violations.

Regular SLA audits help organizations adapt to changing technology, business needs, and user expectations. As new technologies such as cloud computing, AI-driven automation, and remote work solutions emerge, IT teams must reassess SLAs to ensure that they remain relevant. Additionally, periodic user feedback surveys provide insights into whether SLAs align with real-world user expectations, allowing for refinements that enhance service quality.

By implementing effective SLAs, organizations set clear expectations, improve efficiency, enhance accountability, and strengthen relationships between IT teams and end users. These agreements provide a framework for reliable IT service delivery, ensuring that users receive timely support while enabling IT teams to manage resources effectively.

Managing Difficult Users and Handling Complaints

Helpdesk analysts often deal with users who are frustrated, impatient, or uncooperative due to technical problems that disrupt their work. Managing difficult users and handling complaints effectively is a critical skill in IT support, as it helps maintain professionalism, resolve conflicts, and ensure customer satisfaction. While technical knowledge is essential, strong communication, empathy, and problem-solving skills play an equally important role in de-escalating tense situations and maintaining a positive service experience.

One of the most common reasons users become difficult is frustration caused by downtime, data loss, or unresolved technical issues. When users feel that their work has been interrupted, they may direct their anger toward the helpdesk analyst, even if the issue is beyond the analyst's control. In such cases, it is crucial to remain calm, listen actively, and acknowledge the user's frustration. Statements such as 'I understand that this is frustrating for you' or 'I can see why this is causing an inconvenience' help validate the user's feelings and build trust. This approach reassures the user that their concerns are being taken seriously, reducing hostility and opening the door for productive conversation.

Some users may have unrealistic expectations about IT support, expecting immediate solutions for complex issues. If a user demands an urgent fix for a problem that requires time to resolve, it is important to set clear expectations and communicate the estimated resolution time. Instead of saying, 'I don't know when this will be fixed,' a more effective response would be 'I am currently working on the issue, and I expect to have an update for you within the next 30 minutes'. Providing a realistic timeline and keeping users informed of progress helps reduce anxiety and prevents repeated complaints.

Another challenge arises when users blame IT for their mistakes, such as accidentally deleting important files or failing to follow security policies. When handling such complaints, it is important to avoid assigning blame or arguing with the user. A productive approach is to focus on finding a solution rather than dwelling on what went wrong. For example, if a user deleted critical data, instead of saying, 'You should have backed up your files,' a better response would be, 'Let's check if we can recover the files from a backup or restore point'. This keeps the conversation constructive and helps the user see IT as a partner in solving their problem rather than an adversary.

Some users may be difficult due to a lack of technical knowledge, leading to confusion and miscommunication. When dealing with non-technical users, using jargon-free language and explaining steps in simple terms can prevent misunderstandings. Instead of saying, 'Your DNS cache needs to be flushed,' it is more effective to say, 'Your computer may be storing outdated network information. Let's try refreshing it to see if that resolves the issue.' Simplifying technical explanations helps users feel more confident in following instructions and reduces frustration.

In some cases, users may become aggressive or verbally abusive, especially if they feel that their issue is not being resolved quickly enough. When faced with an aggressive user, the most important thing is to remain calm, professional, and composed. Reacting emotionally or defensively can escalate the situation, making it harder to resolve the problem. Instead, responding with neutral and assertive language helps maintain control. If a user raises their voice or becomes rude, responding with 'I'm here to help, and I'd appreciate it if we could keep this conversation respectful' can redirect the discussion in a more productive direction. If the situation continues to escalate, it may be necessary to involve a manager or team lead.

Handling complaints effectively also requires active listening and problem ownership. When a user expresses dissatisfaction with IT services, they want to feel heard and reassured that their concerns matter. Interrupting the user or dismissing their complaint can make the situation worse. Instead, analysts should practice reflective listening, summarizing what the user has said to demonstrate understanding. For example, saying 'If I understand correctly, you've been experiencing slow performance since the last software update, and it's affecting your work. Is that correct?' shows the user that their concern is being taken seriously.

After acknowledging the complaint, taking ownership of the problem and committing to a resolution is essential. Even if the issue is beyond the helpdesk's direct control, reassuring the user with 'I will personally follow up on this and keep you updated' instills confidence that action is being taken. If the complaint involves a repeated issue, escalating it to the appropriate team and ensuring a long-term fix demonstrates a commitment to service improvement.

Some difficult users may be resistant to following troubleshooting steps, insisting that they have already tried everything or refusing to cooperate. In such cases, it is helpful to reframe the troubleshooting process as a collaboration rather than an interrogation. Instead of saying, 'Did you reboot your computer?'—which can sound accusatory—a better approach is, 'Let's try restarting your computer together to see if that clears the issue.' Using inclusive language fosters cooperation and makes the user feel involved in the resolution process.

Providing follow-up communication is another important strategy in handling difficult users. If a complaint has been escalated or requires additional troubleshooting, keeping the user informed of progress prevents frustration. Sending a brief update email or calling the user to check if the issue has been fully resolved demonstrates professionalism and a commitment to customer service. Even after a resolution, following up with 'Is everything working as expected now?' gives the user an opportunity to provide feedback and ensures that no lingering issues remain.

Another aspect of managing difficult users is recognizing when complaints indicate a deeper issue within the IT service process. If multiple users express frustration over slow response times, unclear communication, or recurring technical problems, it may point to a larger systemic issue that needs to be addressed. Gathering feedback from users and analyzing complaint trends can help IT teams identify service gaps, improve response times, and refine support procedures. Proactively improving IT services reduces the likelihood of user dissatisfaction and builds trust between the helpdesk and the organization.

Maintaining a professional and empathetic approach is key to successfully managing difficult users and handling complaints. By remaining patient, listening actively, setting realistic expectations, and communicating clearly, helpdesk analysts can de-escalate conflicts and turn negative interactions into positive experiences. Developing these skills not only improves user satisfaction but also strengthens the overall reputation of the IT support team.

Escalation Procedures and When to Escalate an Issue

In an IT helpdesk environment, escalation procedures ensure that technical issues are resolved efficiently by routing them to the appropriate support level or specialized team. Not all problems can be resolved at the first point of contact, and when an analyst reaches the limits of their knowledge or system access, escalation becomes necessary. Proper escalation procedures help maintain service efficiency, reduce downtime, and improve customer satisfaction by ensuring that complex issues are handled by the right experts. Understanding when and how to escalate an issue is a critical skill for helpdesk analysts, as improper escalation can lead to delays, confusion, and frustrated users.

Escalation typically follows a tiered support structure, where different levels of IT staff handle issues based on complexity and urgency. Tier 1 support is the first line of defense, consisting of helpdesk analysts who resolve common issues such as password resets, basic software troubleshooting, and user access problems. If an issue cannot be resolved at Tier 1 due to its complexity or requirement for system-level changes, it is escalated to Tier 2 support, which consists of more experienced technicians who can handle network troubleshooting, advanced software issues, and system administration tasks. If the issue requires in-depth technical expertise or involves infrastructure failures, it is escalated further to Tier 3 support, which may include server administrators, database specialists, or security teams.

Knowing when to escalate an issue is essential for maintaining efficiency and ensuring that users receive timely resolutions. If a helpdesk analyst has exhausted all available troubleshooting steps and the issue remains unresolved, escalation should be initiated. Repeating the same basic troubleshooting steps without progress wastes both the analyst's and the user's time. Instead, documenting the steps already taken and providing a clear summary of the problem before escalation helps the next level of support address the issue more effectively.

Another key factor in deciding when to escalate is the severity and impact of the issue. IT support teams typically classify incidents based on priority levels, with Priority 1 (P1) issues representing critical outages that affect multiple users or essential business functions. Examples of P1 incidents include company-wide email failures, network outages, and security breaches. These require immediate escalation to senior engineers or incident response teams. Priority 2 (P2) issues involve high-impact problems affecting multiple users but not an entire organization, such as a department-wide application failure. Priority 3 (P3) and Priority 4 (P4) issues are lower-priority concerns, such as individual software bugs or minor system slowdowns, which may not require urgent escalation.

Helpdesk analysts must also recognize when an issue falls outside their scope of responsibility. Some technical problems involve proprietary software, third-party services, or hardware warranties that require vendor assistance. In such cases, escalating the issue to external support teams, vendors, or service providers ensures that the correct specialists handle the request. Before escalating externally, it is essential to gather necessary details such as error logs, screenshots, affected systems, and user impact reports, as third-party support teams often require this information before providing assistance.

The escalation process should always follow a structured workflow to ensure efficiency. When escalating an issue, analysts should provide a clear summary of the problem, steps already taken, error messages encountered, affected systems, and user impact details. Proper documentation prevents redundant troubleshooting and allows the next support level to quickly diagnose the issue. Many helpdesk systems, such as ServiceNow, Jira Service Management, and Zendesk, include built-in escalation workflows that allow analysts to transfer tickets while maintaining visibility into their status.

Effective communication during escalation is critical to maintaining a positive user experience. Users should be informed when their issue is being escalated and provided with an estimated response time, the name of the team handling their request, and any expected follow-up actions. If the resolution process takes longer than expected, updating the user with status reports prevents frustration and ensures transparency. Analysts should avoid simply telling users that their issue is 'being escalated' without context—providing meaningful updates reassures users that progress is being made.

Escalation also applies to non-technical issues, such as policy violations, security concerns, or user behavior problems. If a helpdesk analyst encounters a situation where a user is attempting to bypass security policies, access restricted systems, or requests unauthorized changes, the issue should be escalated to IT management, security teams, or compliance officers. Mishandling such requests can lead to security breaches, data loss, or violations of regulatory requirements.

In addition to incident escalation, helpdesk teams must also handle service request escalations, which involve tasks such as software installations, user permissions, or system access requests. If a request requires manager approval or higher-level IT intervention, following the organization's request approval workflow ensures compliance with company policies. Automating request approvals through identity management systems like Microsoft Active Directory or Okta can streamline the process and reduce delays.

Escalation delays can cause significant productivity loss and frustration among users. To prevent delays, IT teams should establish clear escalation timelines, defining how long an issue should remain at each support tier before being escalated further. For example, a critical network outage may require immediate escalation if not resolved within 30 minutes, while a non-critical software issue may allow up to 24 hours for resolution before escalation. Defining these timeframes in Service Level Agreements (SLAs) helps set user expectations and ensures accountability within IT teams.

One common challenge in escalation is miscommunication between support tiers, which can result in unresolved issues bouncing between teams. To avoid this, analysts should ensure that escalated tickets contain detailed troubleshooting notes, relevant logs, and a clear problem statement. This prevents higher-tier technicians from repeating unnecessary steps and allows them to focus on advanced diagnostics. Collaboration tools such as Microsoft Teams, Slack, or internal chat platforms can also facilitate real-time discussions between support teams, improving the efficiency of escalations.

Escalation procedures should also include post-resolution follow-ups to verify that the issue has been fully addressed. Once an escalated issue is resolved, helpdesk analysts should confirm with the user that the problem has been fixed and document the resolution steps in the ticketing system. This information can later be used to update knowledge base articles, improve troubleshooting guides, and train support staff to handle similar issues without escalation in the future.

Training helpdesk analysts on when and how to escalate effectively is essential for improving service efficiency. New analysts may hesitate to escalate issues for fear of appearing incompetent, while others may escalate too quickly without fully investigating the problem. Encouraging analysts to use internal troubleshooting checklists, knowledge bases, and peer collaboration before escalating ensures that escalations are justified and well-documented.

By implementing structured escalation procedures, IT support teams ensure that technical issues are handled by the right experts, minimizing resolution time and improving overall service quality. Proper escalation management leads to better communication, faster problem resolution, and increased user satisfaction, ultimately contributing to a more efficient and reliable IT support environment.

Asset Management and IT Inventory Control

Asset management and IT inventory control are crucial components of an efficient IT support environment. Keeping track of hardware, software, and other technology assets ensures that organizations can effectively manage resources, reduce costs, and maintain security compliance. Helpdesk analysts play a key role in maintaining accurate records of IT assets, ensuring that devices and software are properly tracked, allocated, and maintained throughout their lifecycle. Effective asset management minimizes risks associated with lost, stolen, or outdated equipment, prevents unauthorized software usage, and improves overall IT operations.

IT asset management (ITAM) encompasses hardware inventory, software license tracking, lifecycle management, procurement, and disposal procedures. Without a structured approach to asset management, organizations risk unnecessary spending on redundant equipment, security vulnerabilities due to outdated devices, and inefficient allocation of IT resources. A well-maintained inventory system allows IT teams to quickly locate assets, track ownership, and manage upgrades or replacements as needed.

One of the most fundamental aspects of IT asset management is hardware tracking, which includes computers, laptops, printers, mobile devices, network infrastructure, and peripherals. Each device should have a unique asset tag or barcode that allows it to be easily identified in the inventory system. These tags are linked to a centralized database that records essential details such as serial numbers, purchase dates, warranty status, assigned users, and last-known locations. Implementing automated asset discovery tools, such as Microsoft System Center Configuration Manager (SCCM), Lansweeper, or SolarWinds, helps IT teams monitor assets in real-time and detect unauthorized devices connected to the network.

Another critical component of asset management is software inventory control, ensuring that organizations comply with software licensing agreements and avoid security risks associated with unapproved applications. Many businesses use Software Asset Management (SAM) tools to track software installations, monitor license usage, and prevent unauthorized software downloads. Unauthorized software can introduce security vulnerabilities, increase the risk of malware infections, and lead to compliance violations with software vendors and regulatory agencies. Keeping software inventories up to date allows IT teams to ensure that all applications are licensed, patched, and properly assigned to users who need them.

Lifecycle management is an essential practice in IT asset management, ensuring that hardware and software are regularly updated, replaced, or retired based on their expected lifespan. IT departments typically follow a refresh cycle, where laptops and desktops are replaced every 3 to 5 years, while network infrastructure and servers may have longer replacement timelines. Tracking the lifecycle of each asset helps organizations plan budget expenditures, avoid sudden hardware failures, and ensure that employees are using up-to-date technology. When an asset reaches the end of its useful life, it must be properly decommissioned, with data securely wiped and hardware recycled or disposed of in accordance with environmental regulations.

One of the biggest challenges in IT inventory control is ensuring that assets are properly assigned to users and departments. Many organizations struggle with ghost assets, which are devices that are listed in inventory but cannot be physically located. This often happens when devices are not properly logged when issued to employees or when employees fail to return equipment upon leaving the company. Maintaining accurate assignment records prevents asset loss and allows IT teams to reclaim and repurpose unused hardware.

Remote work has introduced new challenges for IT asset management, as employees increasingly use company-issued laptops, mobile devices, and peripherals outside the office. Organizations must implement remote asset tracking solutions that allow IT teams to monitor device status, install software updates, and enforce security policies regardless of location. Endpoint management tools like Microsoft Intune, Jamf for macOS devices, and VMware Workspace ONE enable IT teams to maintain control over remote assets, ensuring compliance with corporate security policies.

Security is a major consideration in asset management, as lost or stolen devices can lead to data breaches, unauthorized access, and compliance violations. IT departments should implement encryption, remote wipe capabilities, and device tracking tools to protect sensitive company data. Many organizations use BitLocker (Windows), FileVault (macOS), and mobile device management (MDM) solutions to encrypt data and remotely lock or erase lost devices. Requiring employees to sign asset loan agreements when receiving company-issued devices helps enforce accountability and ensures that equipment is returned when no longer needed.

Auditing and reporting are essential components of an effective IT asset management strategy. Conducting regular inventory audits ensures that asset records remain accurate and up to date. Audits can reveal discrepancies between recorded assets and actual inventory, allowing IT teams to identify missing equipment and ensure compliance with licensing agreements. Many organizations use automated reporting tools to generate detailed reports on asset utilization, maintenance history, and depreciation tracking.

Proper procurement and vendor management also play a role in IT asset management. Organizations must establish standardized purchasing processes to ensure that new IT assets meet corporate requirements and are acquired from approved vendors. Standardization simplifies device maintenance, software compatibility, and security patching. Establishing vendor relationships and service-level agreements (SLAs) helps ensure timely delivery, extended warranties, and efficient support services for IT equipment.

Asset management extends to IT consumables, including keyboards, mice, external hard drives, docking stations, and cables. While these items may seem insignificant compared to servers or workstations, they must be tracked to prevent unnecessary reorders and budget waste. Implementing automated stock replenishment systems ensures that IT teams always have essential accessories available without excessive overstocking.

Cloud asset management is another emerging area of focus, as businesses increasingly rely on cloud computing services such as Microsoft 365, Google Workspace, and Amazon Web Services (AWS). Unlike traditional hardware and software assets, cloud services operate on subscription models, requiring IT teams to track license usage, subscription renewals, and user allocations. Optimizing cloud-based IT spending ensures that organizations do not overpay for unused services while maintaining the necessary capacity for business operations.

Documentation and training are crucial for ensuring that IT asset management processes are consistently followed across the organization. IT teams should maintain detailed asset management policies outlining procedures for asset procurement, allocation, maintenance, tracking, and disposal. Training IT staff and employees on these policies improves compliance and reduces asset loss.

A strong IT asset management strategy optimizes technology usage, reduces costs, enhances security, and ensures compliance with corporate policies. Helpdesk analysts who understand the importance of tracking IT inventory, managing software licenses, securing remote assets, and conducting regular audits contribute to a more efficient and organized IT environment.

Understanding Remote Desktop and Virtual Machines

Remote desktop and virtual machines (VMs) are fundamental technologies that enable users and IT administrators to access and manage computers and servers from a remote location. These technologies are widely used in modern IT environments to provide remote access to corporate systems, support virtualization, and streamline IT management. Helpdesk analysts need to understand how remote desktop connections and virtual machines function, how they are configured, and how to troubleshoot common issues related to these systems. With the growing emphasis on remote work, cloud computing, and virtualization, mastering these concepts is essential for ensuring seamless IT operations.

Remote desktop technology allows a user to connect to a computer or server over a network as if they were physically present at the machine. One of the most widely used remote desktop solutions is Microsoft Remote Desktop Protocol (RDP), which enables Windows users to remotely control another Windows machine. RDP is built into Windows operating systems and can be accessed using the Remote Desktop Connection (mstsc.exe) tool. Other common remote desktop solutions include TeamViewer, AnyDesk, VNC (Virtual Network Computing), and Citrix Virtual Apps and Desktops. These tools allow IT teams to provide remote assistance, troubleshoot problems, and manage servers from anywhere.

When setting up an RDP connection, the target machine must have remote desktop services enabled. In Windows, this can be configured under System Properties > Remote Settings, where users must check the option to allow remote connections. Additionally, the remote computer must have a static IP address or a hostname that can be resolved via DNS. In enterprise environments, RDP connections are typically secured through VPN (Virtual Private Network) access, firewalls, and multi-factor authentication (MFA) to prevent unauthorized access.

One of the most common issues users face when attempting to connect via RDP is the 'Remote Desktop cannot connect to the remote computer' error. This problem can be caused by network connectivity issues, firewall restrictions, incorrect login credentials, or RDP being disabled on the target machine. Helpdesk analysts should first ensure that the remote machine is powered on and accessible by pinging its IP address or hostname. If the machine is reachable, checking whether TCP port 3389 (used by RDP) is open using the telnet command can help determine if the connection is being blocked by a firewall. Additionally, verifying that the user has the correct permissions to access the remote machine under the Remote Desktop Users group is essential for resolving authentication issues.

Security is a critical consideration when using remote desktop services. RDP is a common target for cyberattacks, including brute-force attacks, ransomware deployment, and unauthorized access attempts. Organizations must implement best practices such as using strong passwords, enabling Network Level Authentication (NLA), restricting RDP access to trusted IP addresses, and using Remote Desktop Gateway (RD Gateway) for secure access. Additionally, many businesses implement multi-factor authentication (MFA) for RDP logins to add an extra layer of security.

In addition to remote desktop access, IT teams often use virtual machines (VMs) to create isolated environments for testing, development, and server virtualization. A virtual machine is a software-based emulation of a physical computer, allowing multiple operating systems to run on a single physical machine. Virtual machines are commonly managed using hypervisors, which are software platforms that enable the creation and management of VMs. Popular hypervisors include VMware ESXi, Microsoft Hyper-V, Oracle VirtualBox, and KVM (Kernel-based Virtual Machine) for Linux.

VMs are widely used in enterprise environments for server consolidation, software testing, and disaster recovery. Instead of maintaining separate physical servers for each application, businesses can run multiple virtual machines on a single server, reducing hardware costs and improving resource utilization. Virtualization also enhances scalability, allowing IT teams to quickly deploy new virtual machines without the need for additional physical hardware.

One of the key benefits of using VMs is snapshots and cloning, which allow administrators to take a point-in-time copy of a virtual machine's state. Snapshots are particularly useful for testing new software, applying system updates, and recovering from failed changes. If a critical update causes system instability, the VM can be easily restored to its previous state using a snapshot, minimizing downtime and reducing the risk of data loss.

Helpdesk analysts often assist users with virtual desktop infrastructure (VDI) environments, which allow employees to access a virtualized desktop from any device. VDI solutions such as Citrix Virtual Desktops, VMware Horizon, and Microsoft Azure Virtual Desktop enable organizations to provide centralized desktop environments that can be accessed securely from remote locations. This is particularly beneficial for companies with remote workforces, as it ensures that employees have access to the same corporate applications and data regardless of their physical location.

Troubleshooting virtual machines requires an understanding of resource allocation and performance management. Since multiple VMs run on a single physical host, improper resource allocation can lead to performance issues such as slow processing speeds, high memory usage, and storage bottlenecks. Helpdesk analysts should check CPU, memory, disk, and network utilization to determine whether a VM is under-provisioned or experiencing excessive resource consumption. In environments using VMware or Hyper-V, administrators can adjust virtual CPU (vCPU) and RAM settings to optimize performance.

Another common issue with virtual machines is network connectivity problems, where a VM is unable to communicate with other devices on the network. This can occur due to misconfigured virtual network adapters, incorrect IP configurations, or issues with the virtual switch settings. Checking the VM's network adapter settings in the hypervisor management console and ensuring that it is connected to the correct virtual LAN (VLAN) or bridge network can help resolve these problems. Running ipconfig (Windows) or ifconfig (Linux) within the VM allows analysts to verify its network configuration and troubleshoot connectivity issues.

In cloud environments, virtualization extends beyond on-premises infrastructure to cloud-based virtual machines, such as Amazon EC2 (AWS), Microsoft Azure Virtual Machines, and Google Cloud Compute Engine. These cloud VMs provide scalable, on-demand computing resources that can be used for web hosting, application development, and data processing. IT support teams must understand how to deploy, configure, and secure cloud-based VMs while managing costs and optimizing performance.

Automation plays a significant role in managing VMs and remote desktop environments. Tools such as PowerShell, Ansible, and Terraform allow IT teams to automate VM provisioning, configuration management, and remote desktop access. Using scripts to deploy VMs and manage user access reduces manual workload and ensures consistency across IT infrastructure.

Understanding remote desktop and virtual machines is essential for IT support professionals, as these technologies enable secure remote access, virtualization, and efficient resource management. By mastering RDP troubleshooting, virtualization best practices, and cloud-based VM deployment, helpdesk analysts can enhance IT efficiency and provide seamless support for users in both on-premises and remote environments.

Disaster Recovery and Backup Strategies

Disaster recovery and backup strategies are essential components of IT infrastructure that ensure business continuity in the face of system failures, cyberattacks, natural disasters, or human errors. Organizations rely on well-planned backup and recovery solutions to prevent data loss, minimize downtime, and restore critical systems quickly after an unexpected event. Helpdesk analysts play a crucial role in supporting these strategies by understanding backup technologies, troubleshooting data restoration issues, and ensuring that disaster recovery plans are effectively implemented.

A well-defined disaster recovery plan (DRP) outlines the processes and procedures that an organization must follow to recover IT systems and data after an outage or disaster. The primary goal of disaster recovery is to restore business operations as quickly and efficiently as possible while minimizing the impact on users and customers. A DRP typically includes risk assessments, recovery time objectives (RTO), recovery point objectives (RPO), backup retention policies, failover procedures, and testing protocols.

Recovery Time Objective (RTO) and Recovery Point Objective (RPO) are two critical metrics in disaster recovery planning. RTO defines the maximum acceptable downtime for a system before it begins to significantly impact business operations. For example, a company may set an RTO of four hours for a critical database server, meaning that IT teams must restore the system within that timeframe. RPO, on the other hand, determines the maximum acceptable data loss measured in time. If an RPO is set at one hour, backups must be performed frequently enough to ensure that no more than one hour of data is lost in the event of a failure. Lower RTOs and RPOs require more advanced backup and replication technologies, increasing costs but ensuring faster recovery.

Organizations use a variety of backup methods to protect data and ensure recoverability. One of the most common approaches is full backups, where all selected files and system data are copied to a backup destination. Full backups provide the most comprehensive protection but require significant storage space and time to complete. To optimize storage and backup efficiency, many organizations use incremental and differential backups. Incremental backups only store the data that has changed since the last backup, reducing storage requirements but requiring multiple backup sets for full restoration. Differential backups, in contrast, store all changes made since the last full backup, allowing for faster restoration compared to incremental backups while using more storage space.

Modern backup strategies also include image-based backups and file-based backups. Image-based backups create a complete snapshot of a system, including the operating system, applications, and configurations. This method allows IT teams to quickly restore entire systems to a functional state after a hardware failure or cyberattack. File-based backups, on the other hand, focus on individual files and folders, making them more suitable for data protection rather than full system recovery. Many organizations implement hybrid backup strategies that combine both approaches to ensure comprehensive protection.

Storage locations for backups vary based on business needs, security requirements, and regulatory compliance. On-premises backups store copies of data locally, often on network-attached storage (NAS) devices, external hard drives, or tape libraries. While on-premises backups provide fast recovery times, they are vulnerable to physical damage from disasters such as fires or floods. Cloud backups, on the other hand, offer offsite protection by storing data in secure data centers operated by cloud providers such as AWS, Microsoft Azure, or Google Cloud. Cloud backups provide geographical redundancy, scalability, and disaster resilience, making them a popular choice for modern enterprises.

For organizations that require high availability, real-time replication and failover solutions ensure continuous access to critical systems. Technologies such as RAID (Redundant Array of Independent Disks), database replication, and site-to-site mirroring allow businesses to maintain live copies of data across multiple locations. High availability clusters, such as VMware vSphere High Availability (HA) and Microsoft Failover Clustering, automatically transfer workloads to backup systems in the event of a failure, reducing downtime.

Cybersecurity threats such as ransomware attacks have increased the importance of immutable backups that cannot be altered or deleted by malware. Organizations use air-gapped backups, which are physically disconnected from the network, to prevent cybercriminals from encrypting or destroying backup data. Many backup solutions also offer versioning, allowing IT teams to restore previous file versions that were unaffected by ransomware or accidental deletions.

Testing and validation are crucial aspects of disaster recovery planning. Many organizations schedule regular disaster recovery drills to ensure that backup systems function correctly and that IT teams can execute recovery procedures efficiently. Without proper testing, businesses may discover backup failures, corrupted data, or misconfigured restore settings only when a real disaster occurs. IT teams use sandbox environments to simulate system failures and validate recovery times without affecting production systems.

Compliance and regulatory requirements also play a significant role in backup strategies. Many industries, including finance, healthcare, and government agencies, must adhere to strict data retention policies outlined in regulations such as GDPR, HIPAA, and SOX. These regulations specify how long data must be retained, where it can be stored, and how it must be protected. Organizations must ensure that their backup solutions comply with these legal requirements to avoid penalties and maintain data integrity.

Automation enhances backup efficiency by reducing human errors and ensuring consistency. IT teams use automated backup scheduling to run backups at predefined intervals without manual intervention. Backup management tools such as Veeam, Acronis, Commvault, and Backup Exec provide centralized control over backup policies, encryption settings, and recovery workflows. Monitoring and alerting mechanisms notify IT teams of failed backup jobs, ensuring prompt corrective action.

Helpdesk analysts play a crucial role in assisting users with backup-related issues, such as restoring lost files, verifying backup availability, and troubleshooting failed backup jobs. When users accidentally delete files or experience data corruption, analysts must quickly determine whether a backup exists and guide the user through the restoration process. If a backup job fails, analysts must diagnose the cause by reviewing backup logs, checking storage availability, and verifying network connectivity.

Disaster recovery planning extends beyond data backups to include strategies for restoring network infrastructure, virtual machines, and cloud environments. Many organizations use Disaster Recovery as a Service (DRaaS) to replicate entire IT environments in the cloud, allowing businesses to quickly resume operations after a major disruption. Cloud-based disaster recovery solutions eliminate the need for costly secondary data centers while ensuring scalability and rapid failover.

A well-structured backup and disaster recovery strategy ensures that organizations can recover quickly from system failures, cyber threats, or natural disasters. By implementing redundant backup systems, testing recovery procedures, and maintaining compliance with regulatory requirements, businesses minimize risks and safeguard their critical data. Helpdesk analysts who understand backup technologies, troubleshooting methodologies, and disaster recovery principles contribute significantly to an organization's ability to respond to emergencies and maintain business continuity.

Multi-Factor Authentication (MFA) and Security Policies

Multi-Factor Authentication (MFA) is a critical security measure that enhances user authentication by requiring multiple forms of verification before granting access to an account or system. Traditional authentication methods rely solely on passwords, which are susceptible to theft, brute-force attacks, and social engineering tactics. By implementing MFA, organizations significantly reduce the risk of unauthorized access, protecting sensitive information and ensuring compliance with security best practices.

MFA operates by requiring users to present two or more verification factors before gaining access to a system. These authentication factors are typically categorized into three types: something you know, something you have, and something you are. The 'something you know' factor refers to passwords, PINs, or security questions. The 'something you have' factor includes physical or digital tokens, such as security keys, smart cards, or authentication apps. The 'something you are' factor is based on biometric data, such as fingerprints, facial recognition, or retina scans. By combining at least two of these factors, MFA strengthens authentication security and makes it more difficult for attackers to compromise accounts.

One of the most commonly used MFA methods involves authentication apps, such as Microsoft Authenticator, Google Authenticator, and Duo Security. These apps generate time-based one-time passwords (TOTP) that users must enter in addition to their regular credentials. Since these codes expire after a short period, attackers who steal a password cannot gain access without also having the MFA code. Many organizations also use SMS-based MFA, where a one-time passcode is sent via text message. While SMS authentication provides an additional layer of security, it is more vulnerable to SIM swapping attacks and interception than app-based authentication. For higher security, organizations often prefer hardware-based security keys, such as YubiKey or Titan Security Key, which provide cryptographic authentication and are resistant to phishing attempts.

MFA plays a vital role in Zero Trust Security, an approach that assumes no user or device should be trusted by default, even if they are inside the corporate network. Organizations implementing Zero Trust require users to verify their identity using MFA every time they attempt to access critical systems, rather than relying on traditional network-based access controls. This minimizes the risk of lateral movement in case of a compromised account.

While MFA enhances security, it is most effective when combined with comprehensive security policies that govern authentication, access control, and data protection. Security policies define the rules and best practices that users must follow to protect organizational assets. One of the most important policies related to MFA is the password policy, which sets guidelines for password complexity, expiration, and reuse. Many organizations enforce strong password policies, requiring users to create passwords with a mix of uppercase and lowercase letters, numbers, and special characters. Additionally, password rotation policies prevent users from reusing old passwords, reducing the likelihood of credential-based attacks.

Security policies also cover account lockout mechanisms, which prevent brute-force attacks by locking an account after multiple failed login attempts. A common policy is to lock accounts after five incorrect password entries and require either a cooling-off period or manual intervention by IT support to restore access. Combining account lockouts with MFA ensures that even if an attacker guesses a password, they cannot bypass the additional verification step.

Another critical security policy involves privileged access management (PAM), which restricts access to sensitive systems based on user roles and responsibilities. IT administrators, executives, and employees with access to confidential information should be required to use stronger authentication methods, such as MFA with biometric verification or physical security keys. Many organizations implement role-based access control (RBAC) to enforce least privilege access, ensuring that users only have the permissions necessary for their job functions.

Security awareness training is an essential component of MFA and security policies. Many successful cyberattacks occur due to phishing scams, credential theft, or social engineering tactics that trick users into revealing authentication details. Employees should be educated on how to recognize phishing emails, avoid clicking on suspicious links, and verify MFA prompts to prevent unauthorized access. Attackers frequently use MFA fatigue attacks, where they bombard a user with multiple MFA prompts in an attempt to trick them into approving an unauthorized login. IT teams should implement MFA policies that limit repeated authentication attempts and notify users of suspicious login activity.

Another key security policy is device and endpoint security, which ensures that MFA-protected accounts are not accessed from compromised devices. Organizations use Mobile Device Management (MDM) and Endpoint Detection and Response (EDR) solutions to enforce security policies on corporate devices. These policies may include blocking MFA approvals from jailbroken or rooted phones, requiring device encryption, and enforcing compliance checks before granting access. If a device fails a compliance check, access to company resources can be automatically revoked until security issues are resolved.

MFA is also widely used in cloud security policies to protect Microsoft 365, Google Workspace, AWS, and other cloud-based applications. Many cloud providers offer Conditional Access Policies, which allow IT teams to enforce MFA based on specific conditions, such as location, device type, or risk score. For example, an organization might require MFA only when users log in from an unfamiliar device or outside the corporate network. This adaptive approach reduces friction for users while maintaining security.

Security policies should also define incident response procedures for compromised MFA accounts. If an attacker gains access to a user's primary login credentials and attempts to bypass MFA, organizations must have a clear protocol for resetting MFA settings, revoking active sessions, and investigating potential breaches. Many IT teams use Security Information and Event Management (SIEM) solutions to monitor authentication logs and detect anomalies, such as multiple failed MFA attempts from different geographic locations.

Regular audits and compliance checks ensure that MFA and security policies remain effective over time. Organizations must periodically review MFA adoption rates, security policy compliance, and access logs to identify weaknesses. Regulatory frameworks such as NIST, GDPR, HIPAA, and PCI-DSS require businesses to implement MFA as part of their security compliance obligations. Failure to enforce proper security policies can lead to data breaches, financial penalties, and reputational damage.

Helpdesk analysts play a key role in MFA support and security enforcement, assisting users with setting up MFA, troubleshooting authentication errors, and responding to security alerts. One of the most common support requests involves users losing access to their MFA devices. IT teams should establish secure recovery options, such as backup authentication methods, one-time recovery codes, or administrator-approved resets. However, recovery policies must be carefully designed to prevent attackers from exploiting account recovery mechanisms as a way to bypass MFA.

Organizations adopting MFA and strong security policies benefit from greater protection against credential theft, phishing attacks, and unauthorized access. By enforcing best practices such as adaptive MFA, role-based access controls, and security awareness training, businesses can ensure that their authentication mechanisms remain resilient against evolving cyber threats. Helpdesk analysts and IT security teams must work together to continuously refine authentication policies, monitor for security risks, and provide user support to maintain a secure and efficient authentication framework.

Working with Different IT Teams: Collaboration and Coordination

Effective collaboration between IT teams is essential for maintaining a seamless and efficient technology environment. The modern IT infrastructure consists of multiple specialized teams, each responsible for different aspects of technology management, including helpdesk support, network administration, cybersecurity, system administration, cloud computing, software development, and database management. Helpdesk analysts often serve as the first point of contact for technical issues, making their ability to coordinate with other IT teams crucial for ensuring timely problem resolution and maintaining business continuity.

One of the primary responsibilities of a helpdesk analyst is to accurately diagnose and categorize issues before escalating them to the appropriate IT team. Not all issues can be resolved at the first level of support, and escalating tickets without proper documentation or initial troubleshooting can lead to inefficiencies. To streamline collaboration, helpdesk analysts must provide detailed problem descriptions, logs, screenshots, and the troubleshooting steps already taken before passing an issue to another team. This reduces redundant efforts, prevents miscommunication, and helps specialized IT teams focus on complex problem resolution rather than repeating basic troubleshooting steps.

The network administration team is responsible for managing the organization's network infrastructure, including routers, switches, firewalls, VPNs, and wireless networks. Helpdesk analysts frequently coordinate with network administrators to address connectivity issues, slow internet speeds, VPN access problems, and firewall restrictions. When troubleshooting network-related problems, analysts should first perform basic diagnostics, such as running ping, tracert, or nslookup commands, before escalating the issue. Providing network logs, IP addresses, and error messages helps network administrators quickly identify and resolve the root cause of the problem.

Collaboration with the cybersecurity team is essential for maintaining a secure IT environment. Helpdesk analysts play a frontline role in identifying and reporting potential security threats, such as phishing emails, malware infections, or unauthorized access attempts. If a user reports suspicious activity on their account, helpdesk analysts should gather login timestamps, device details, and recent activity logs before escalating the case to the cybersecurity team. Additionally, analysts assist in enforcing security policies, such as multi-factor authentication (MFA) setup, account lockout procedures, and security awareness training. Working closely with cybersecurity professionals helps organizations proactively address security incidents and prevent data breaches.

The system administration team manages Windows and Linux servers, Active Directory, group policies, and user access control. Helpdesk analysts frequently work with system administrators to handle account creation, password resets, folder permissions, software deployments, and server outages. When escalating system-related issues, analysts should provide user account details, affected system names, and error logs to help system administrators diagnose and resolve the problem efficiently. System administrators also rely on helpdesk teams to enforce IT policies, ensuring that users comply with corporate security guidelines and access control rules.

In modern IT environments, cloud computing teams manage infrastructure hosted on platforms such as Amazon Web Services (AWS), Microsoft Azure, and Google Cloud. Many businesses rely on cloud-based services for virtual machines, storage, databases, and applications, requiring helpdesk analysts to coordinate with cloud engineers when users experience login failures, application downtime, or cloud resource access issues. When escalating cloud-related tickets, analysts should verify whether the issue is specific to a user or system-wide and include relevant cloud service logs, error messages, and configuration details to help cloud teams troubleshoot efficiently.

Collaboration with the software development team is necessary when users encounter bugs, crashes, or compatibility issues with internal applications. Helpdesk analysts must differentiate between user errors, system misconfigurations, and actual software defects before involving developers. Gathering detailed reproduction steps, affected application versions, and user impact reports helps developers identify and fix issues more quickly. Many organizations use ticketing systems such as Jira, ServiceNow, or Zendesk to track software bugs and ensure that developers receive complete information when a ticket is escalated.

The database administration (DBA) team is responsible for managing SQL and NoSQL databases, optimizing performance, ensuring data integrity, and handling backup and recovery. Helpdesk analysts often need to coordinate with database administrators when users report slow database queries, missing records, or permission errors in enterprise applications. Before escalating, analysts should verify whether the issue is related to application settings, user access permissions, or actual database corruption. Providing query execution times, error messages, and recent database changes helps DBAs diagnose and resolve issues effectively.

Effective communication is the key to successful collaboration between IT teams. Using structured communication channels, such as internal chat platforms (Microsoft Teams, Slack, or Mattermost), shared documentation, and email ticketing systems, ensures that information is accurate, transparent, and easily accessible. Helpdesk analysts should clearly document ticket updates, issue resolution progress, and user communications to maintain accountability and facilitate knowledge sharing.

Regular cross-team meetings, training sessions, and technical workshops help IT teams align their efforts and improve coordination. When helpdesk analysts understand the responsibilities and workflows of network engineers, system administrators, cybersecurity teams, and developers, they can escalate issues more effectively and reduce resolution times. Encouraging IT teams to share best practices, troubleshooting techniques, and emerging technologies fosters a collaborative culture that benefits the entire organization.

Standardizing incident response and escalation procedures is another important aspect of IT team collaboration. Many organizations use ITIL (Information Technology Infrastructure Library) frameworks to define clear escalation paths, service level agreements (SLAs), and response time objectives. When a major incident occurs, IT teams must work together to prioritize tasks, communicate updates to stakeholders, and restore services as quickly as possible. Helpdesk analysts play a crucial role in incident documentation, user communication, and coordinating between different IT teams during critical outages.

Technical documentation and knowledge sharing also improve interdepartmental coordination. Maintaining an internal knowledge base, troubleshooting guides, and standard operating procedures (SOPs) ensures that IT teams have access to consistent and well-documented solutions. Helpdesk analysts should regularly update knowledge base articles based on recurring issues, new system configurations, and lessons learned from past incidents.

The ability to collaborate effectively across IT teams enhances overall efficiency, reduces response times, and improves user satisfaction. Helpdesk analysts who develop strong communication skills, document issues clearly, and proactively engage with other IT professionals contribute significantly to the success of IT operations. By fostering a culture of teamwork, knowledge sharing, and structured coordination, organizations create a resilient and agile IT environment capable of addressing technical challenges, security threats, and business demands efficiently.

Time Management and Prioritization Skills

Time management and prioritization are essential skills for helpdesk analysts, as they must handle multiple tasks simultaneously while ensuring timely resolution of technical issues. An efficient IT support environment requires analysts to manage their workload effectively, meet service level agreements (SLAs), and maintain high levels of customer satisfaction. Without proper time management, analysts can quickly become overwhelmed, leading to longer response times, unresolved issues, and increased frustration among users. Developing strong prioritization skills allows helpdesk professionals to allocate their time wisely, focus on the most critical issues first, and balance urgent tasks with long-term projects.

One of the primary challenges in helpdesk support is managing an unpredictable workload. New tickets arrive constantly, and some require immediate attention, while others can be addressed later. Analysts must assess each request based on urgency, impact, and complexity to determine the appropriate priority level. A priority matrix is a useful tool for categorizing tasks based on two factors: importance and urgency. Urgent and high-impact issues, such as network outages or security incidents, should be addressed immediately, while low-priority requests, such as routine software installations or minor UI bugs, can be scheduled for later resolution.

Service Level Agreements (SLAs) provide a structured framework for prioritization. Most organizations define target response and resolution times based on issue severity. For example, a critical system failure affecting multiple users may have a resolution time of two hours, while a non-urgent software request may have a response time of 24 hours. Helpdesk analysts must be familiar with SLA requirements and ensure that they prioritize tickets accordingly to meet company-wide service commitments.

Effective ticket triaging plays a key role in managing time efficiently. When a new ticket is received, the analyst should first determine whether it is a quick fix, a complex issue requiring escalation, or a request that can be handled later. Simple issues, such as password resets or printer errors, should be resolved immediately to prevent unnecessary backlog. More complex problems, such as database failures or system crashes, may require collaboration with other IT teams. Proper ticket categorization ensures that resources are allocated efficiently and that urgent requests do not get lost among lower-priority tasks.

Managing interruptions and distractions is another critical aspect of time management. Helpdesk analysts often face constant interruptions from phone calls, emails, chat messages, and walk-in requests. While providing support is the primary responsibility, frequent distractions can reduce efficiency and cause delays in resolving critical issues. One strategy to minimize disruptions is to establish designated focus times for handling high-priority tickets without interruption. Additionally, using automated responses and self-service resources can help reduce unnecessary inquiries, allowing analysts to focus on more complex tasks.

Multitasking is often seen as a necessary skill in IT support, but it can also lead to inefficiencies if not managed properly. Switching between multiple tasks too frequently can reduce productivity and increase the likelihood of errors. Instead of attempting to resolve multiple issues at once, analysts should use task batching, where similar tasks are grouped together and completed in a single session. For example, instead of handling password resets sporadically throughout the day, an analyst could dedicate specific time slots to process all pending account-related requests at once.

A structured daily workflow helps analysts allocate their time more effectively. A typical workflow may include checking and categorizing new tickets at the start of the shift, resolving quick fixes, prioritizing critical issues, handling scheduled maintenance tasks, and conducting follow-ups with users. Using a to-do list or task management system, such as Trello, Asana, or Microsoft Planner, can help keep track of ongoing responsibilities and deadlines. Setting realistic time estimates for each task ensures that workloads remain manageable and that important issues do not fall behind schedule.

Documentation plays a crucial role in improving time management. Keeping clear and detailed records of resolved issues, troubleshooting steps, and system configurations allows analysts to quickly refer back to past solutions without repeating the same investigative process. A knowledge base of common issues and resolutions can also help reduce ticket volume by providing self-service options for users. When a user encounters a recurring problem, referring them to a well-documented solution saves time for both the analyst and the end user.

Proactive planning and anticipating potential issues can help reduce the number of reactive support requests. Regular system monitoring, preventive maintenance, and software updates can prevent common technical issues before they escalate into major incidents. By staying ahead of known problems, analysts can reduce the frequency of emergency escalations and allocate more time to long-term IT improvements.

Managing user expectations is another key component of effective time management. Users often expect immediate resolution to their issues, even when a request is low priority. Clear communication about estimated resolution times, current ticket backlog, and escalation procedures helps users understand when they can expect a response. Providing status updates on high-priority tickets reassures users that their issues are being actively worked on, reducing unnecessary follow-ups and duplicate requests.

Collaboration with other IT teams is also essential for time efficiency. Some issues require assistance from network engineers, system administrators, or developers, and coordinating effectively ensures that escalations are handled promptly. When escalating a ticket, analysts should provide detailed logs, troubleshooting notes, and relevant system information to prevent delays caused by missing or incomplete data. Effective communication between teams reduces resolution time and prevents repeated investigations into the same issue.

Time management is not just about handling daily tasks efficiently—it also involves continuous learning and skill development. Helpdesk analysts should set aside time for training, certifications, and learning new technologies to stay updated with industry trends. Investing in professional development helps analysts resolve issues more quickly and expand their technical expertise, reducing reliance on escalations.

Stress management and avoiding burnout are also important aspects of time management. Constant pressure to meet deadlines, handle multiple requests, and respond to urgent issues can lead to mental fatigue and decreased productivity. Taking short breaks, practicing workload balance, and using stress reduction techniques can help analysts maintain long-term efficiency and job satisfaction. Encouraging a supportive team environment where colleagues assist each other during high workloads improves overall morale and productivity.

Developing strong time management and prioritization skills allows helpdesk analysts to work more efficiently, meet SLA commitments, and ensure that users receive timely technical support. By using structured workflows, task prioritization techniques, and effective communication strategies, IT professionals can manage their workload effectively, reduce response times, and maintain high-quality service delivery.

Dealing with High Ticket Volume and Stress Management

Working in a helpdesk or service desk environment often means handling a high volume of support tickets daily. The constant influx of user requests, system issues, and urgent escalations can create overwhelming workloads for IT analysts. When ticket volumes are high, maintaining efficiency, accuracy, and a professional attitude becomes more challenging. Additionally, prolonged exposure to high-pressure situations can lead to stress, burnout, and decreased productivity. Developing effective strategies to manage high ticket volumes while maintaining mental well-being is essential for success in an IT support role.

One of the first steps in managing a high ticket volume is prioritization. Not all tickets require the same level of urgency, and helpdesk analysts must learn to quickly categorize issues based on their impact and severity. Critical issues, such as network outages, server failures, or security breaches, should take top priority, as they affect multiple users or business operations. High-priority tickets include issues that significantly impact a single user's ability to work, such as account lockouts or application crashes. Lower-priority tickets, such as minor software bugs or general inquiries, should be addressed when time allows but should not take precedence over urgent matters. Using a structured priority matrix ensures that the most critical tasks receive immediate attention, while less urgent issues are scheduled appropriately.

Ticket triaging is an essential skill when dealing with high volumes. Instead of handling tickets in the order they arrive, analysts should quickly assess each ticket, determine the category, and route it to the appropriate resolution path. Some tickets can be resolved instantly with a simple fix, while others require in-depth troubleshooting or escalation to specialized IT teams. Implementing an automated ticketing system that categorizes and assigns tickets based on predefined rules helps reduce manual workload and ensures that tickets are handled by the right team members.

Self-service solutions are another effective way to reduce ticket volume. Many helpdesk tickets involve repetitive issues, such as password resets, printer connectivity problems, or basic software troubleshooting. Organizations can implement knowledge bases, FAQ sections, and automated chatbots to allow users to find answers to common problems without submitting a ticket. When users are encouraged to check self-service options before contacting the helpdesk, analysts can focus on more complex issues that require technical expertise.

Efficiency also depends on standardized responses and scripts for common issues. Instead of writing the same troubleshooting steps repeatedly, analysts should maintain a library of prewritten responses and macros that can be quickly inserted into tickets. Many ticketing systems, such as Zendesk, ServiceNow, and Freshdesk, allow for the creation of canned responses that speed up ticket resolution while maintaining consistency in support. Analysts can modify these responses as needed to personalize communication with users.

Managing time effectively is critical when dealing with a high workload. Analysts should use time-blocking techniques to allocate dedicated periods for responding to tickets, handling escalations, and following up on pending issues. Avoiding constant task-switching minimizes distractions and helps maintain focus on high-priority tickets. Additionally, setting realistic time estimates for each ticket type helps analysts avoid spending too much time on a single issue while other tickets pile up.

Collaboration with other IT teams can help alleviate pressure during peak ticket volumes. If the helpdesk is overwhelmed with requests, distributing tickets to system administrators, network engineers, or security teams ensures that issues are handled efficiently. Creating a clear escalation process prevents bottlenecks and ensures that analysts can offload tasks that require specialized expertise rather than attempting to resolve everything alone.

High ticket volumes can create a stressful work environment, leading to fatigue, frustration, and burnout. Learning to manage stress is just as important as technical skills in IT support. One of the most effective ways to reduce stress is to focus on what can be controlled. Analysts cannot prevent system outages, user frustrations, or sudden spikes in ticket requests, but they can control their response, workload organization, and problem-solving approach. Practicing mindfulness and maintaining a positive attitude helps prevent negative emotions from affecting performance.

Taking regular breaks is essential to prevent mental exhaustion. Short breaks between tasks help reset focus and maintain productivity throughout the day. Many analysts fall into the habit of working through lunch or skipping breaks to keep up with ticket volume, but this often leads to increased fatigue and reduced problem-solving ability. Even a five-minute break to stretch, take a walk, or disconnect from screens can help restore mental clarity and prevent stress buildup.

Workload balance is another critical factor in long-term stress management. If an analyst is consistently handling more tickets than the team average, it may indicate uneven task distribution or a lack of sufficient staffing. IT managers should regularly review workload distribution and reassign tasks if necessary. Encouraging team collaboration and peer support ensures that no individual analyst becomes overwhelmed.

Developing emotional resilience is also necessary for managing stress. Helpdesk analysts frequently deal with frustrated, impatient, or demanding users, and it's easy to take negative interactions personally. Learning to separate user frustration from personal identity helps analysts remain calm and professional in difficult situations. Practicing active listening, empathy, and clear communication helps de-escalate conflicts and improves the overall support experience for both users and analysts.

Keeping a log of achievements and successes can boost morale and motivation. When dealing with an overwhelming workload, it's easy to focus on unfinished tasks rather than recognizing accomplishments. Keeping track of resolved tickets, positive user feedback, or difficult issues that were successfully fixed provides a sense of progress and helps maintain motivation.

Work-life balance is another important consideration. Bringing work-related stress home can negatively impact personal well-being and relationships. Establishing clear boundaries between work and personal time ensures that stress does not carry over after working hours. Engaging in hobbies, exercise, or relaxation activities outside of work helps create a healthier balance and prevents burnout.

Another effective strategy for stress management is continuous learning and professional growth. When analysts develop their technical skills, problem-solving abilities, and industry knowledge, they become more confident and efficient, reducing the stress associated with complex or unfamiliar issues. Pursuing IT certifications, attending training sessions, and staying updated on new technologies can enhance efficiency and provide long-term career benefits.

Finally, fostering a supportive team culture helps reduce stress in high-pressure environments. Encouraging team members to share knowledge, assist each other, and provide emotional support creates a positive work environment where analysts feel valued and supported. Teams that communicate openly and celebrate successes together are better equipped to handle demanding workloads.

Dealing with high ticket volumes and managing stress effectively requires a combination of prioritization, time management, collaboration, and self-care strategies. Helpdesk analysts who develop these skills can maintain productivity, reduce burnout, and provide high-quality technical support even in challenging work environments. By balancing efficiency with well-being, IT professionals create a sustainable and rewarding career in technical support.

Career Growth: Certifications and Professional Development

Building a successful career as a helpdesk or service desk analyst requires continuous learning, skill development, and professional growth. The IT industry evolves rapidly, with new technologies, security threats, and best practices emerging regularly. Helpdesk analysts who actively pursue certifications, training, and career development opportunities increase their chances of advancing into higher-paying roles, such as system administrator, network engineer, cybersecurity analyst, or IT manager. Investing in professional development not only enhances technical expertise but also improves problem-solving skills, confidence, and job satisfaction.

One of the most effective ways to advance in an IT career is by earning industry-recognized certifications. Certifications validate technical knowledge and demonstrate a commitment to professional growth.

Employers often look for candidates with relevant certifications, as they provide assurance that the individual has met a standardized level of competence. The most valuable certifications for helpdesk analysts depend on their career goals and areas of interest.

For those starting in IT support, the CompTIA A+ certification is one of the most widely recognized credentials. It covers hardware troubleshooting, operating systems, networking fundamentals, and security basics, making it an excellent starting point for entry-level IT professionals. Many employers require or prefer A+ certification for helpdesk and technical support roles, as it ensures a foundational understanding of computer systems and IT infrastructure.

Beyond the A+ certification, helpdesk analysts looking to advance into networking roles should consider the CompTIA Network+ or Cisco Certified Network Associate (CCNA) certifications. Network+ covers essential networking concepts, such as IP addressing, routing, switching, and troubleshooting connectivity issues, making it valuable for those interested in supporting networked environments. The CCNA goes a step further, focusing on Cisco networking technologies, VLANs, WANs, and security protocols. These certifications are beneficial for helpdesk analysts who frequently troubleshoot network-related issues or aspire to become network administrators.

For those interested in cybersecurity, the CompTIA Security+ certification is an excellent choice. Security+ covers risk management, encryption, access control, threat detection, and incident response, providing a strong foundation for IT professionals looking to move into security-focused roles. As cyber threats continue to grow, organizations increasingly seek IT staff with security expertise, making Security+ a valuable credential for career advancement. Those wanting to specialize further in security can pursue more advanced certifications, such as Certified Ethical Hacker (CEH), GIAC Security Essentials (GSEC), or Certified Information Systems Security Professional (CISSP).

Microsoft certifications are also highly beneficial for helpdesk analysts working in Windows-based environments. The Microsoft 365 Certified: Modern Desktop Administrator Associate certification validates skills in Windows 10 and 11 management, endpoint security, and cloud-based services, making it ideal for analysts supporting enterprise users. Those working with Microsoft Active Directory, cloud solutions, or enterprise applications may benefit from Microsoft Certified: Azure Fundamentals or Azure Administrator Associate, which focus on Microsoft's cloud platform and identity management solutions.

In addition to technical certifications, helpdesk analysts should develop soft skills and leadership abilities to enhance their career prospects. Effective communication, customer service, time management, and teamwork are essential for success in IT support roles. Many organizations offer ITIL (Information Technology Infrastructure Library) certifications, which focus on IT service management (ITSM) best practices. The ITIL Foundation certification is particularly valuable for helpdesk analysts, as it teaches incident management, problem resolution, change control, and service delivery strategies.

Professional development goes beyond certifications and includes hands-on experience, mentorship, and networking opportunities. Helpdesk analysts should seek out challenging projects, cross-team collaborations, and internal training programs to expand their knowledge and demonstrate initiative. Many organizations encourage shadowing senior IT staff or participating in interdepartmental meetings to gain exposure to system administration, cybersecurity, cloud management, and infrastructure planning.

Attending industry conferences, webinars, and networking events is another excellent way to stay informed about emerging technologies, best practices, and career opportunities. Events such as Black Hat, DEF CON, Microsoft Ignite, Cisco Live, and AWS re:Invent provide valuable insights into industry trends and allow IT professionals to connect with peers, recruiters, and hiring managers. Engaging with online communities, such as Reddit's r/sysadmin, Spiceworks, or LinkedIn IT groups, also helps professionals stay updated on IT challenges, solutions, and career development tips.

Helpdesk analysts who aspire to move into system administration, cloud engineering, or DevOps roles should gain hands-on experience with virtualization, automation, and scripting. Learning PowerShell, Bash scripting, and Python can greatly enhance efficiency in IT operations, allowing professionals to automate repetitive tasks, manage user accounts, and configure systems programmatically. Many free and paid online platforms, such as Pluralsight, Udemy, Coursera, and Microsoft Learn, offer courses on scripting, cloud computing, and infrastructure automation.

For those interested in cloud technologies, gaining familiarity with platforms like Amazon Web Services (AWS), Microsoft Azure, and Google Cloud Platform (GCP) can open doors to high-demand cloud engineering roles. Entry-level cloud certifications, such as AWS Certified Cloud Practitioner or Microsoft Certified: Azure Fundamentals, provide a strong foundation for IT professionals transitioning into cloud computing. As more organizations migrate to the cloud, hybrid IT skills that combine traditional infrastructure knowledge with cloud expertise are becoming increasingly valuable.

Mentorship and career coaching can also accelerate professional development. Finding a mentor within the IT department, an online community, or a professional association provides valuable guidance on career paths, skills development, and industry insights. Mentors can help junior IT professionals navigate career transitions, prepare for technical interviews, and identify areas for improvement. Many organizations also offer internal career development programs, where employees can set long-term career goals and receive structured support from IT leadership.

For long-term career growth, helpdesk analysts should actively seek promotion opportunities within their organization. Moving from Tier 1 support to Tier 2 or Tier 3 roles often involves developing deeper expertise in networking, system administration, cybersecurity, or cloud technologies. Analysts should volunteer for high-visibility projects, demonstrate leadership in incident resolution, and showcase their ability to handle complex IT challenges. Regularly updating one's resume, preparing for internal job openings, and staying proactive in skill development can significantly accelerate career progression.

Building a strong personal brand as an IT professional is another key aspect of career development. Maintaining an up-to-date LinkedIn profile, contributing to IT forums, writing technical blog posts, or participating in open-source projects can help professionals establish credibility and increase job market visibility. Many hiring managers look for candidates with demonstrated expertise, a strong professional network, and a willingness to share knowledge.

The IT field is highly dynamic, competitive, and constantly evolving, making continuous learning a necessity for career advancement. Helpdesk analysts who pursue certifications, hands-on experience, leadership development, and networking opportunities position themselves for long-term success. By proactively expanding their technical skills, soft skills, and professional connections, IT professionals can move beyond entry-level support roles and advance into specialized, high-paying positions in network administration, cybersecurity, cloud computing, DevOps, and IT management.

Building a Professional Resume and Interview Tips

A well-structured resume and strong interview skills are essential for advancing a career in IT support and securing a helpdesk or service desk analyst position. In the competitive job market, a resume serves as the first impression for hiring managers, highlighting technical skills, experience, and qualifications. A strong resume increases the likelihood of securing an interview, while effective interview techniques demonstrate problem-solving abilities, communication skills, and technical knowledge. Helpdesk analysts must focus on both resume-building and interview preparation to stand out among candidates and position themselves for career growth.

A professional resume should be clear, concise, and tailored to the specific role. Hiring managers often scan resumes quickly, so presenting key qualifications in an easy-to-read format increases the chances of being shortlisted. The resume should begin with a summary or objective statement that briefly describes experience, skills, and career goals. For example, an entry-level IT support professional might write:

'Motivated IT support specialist with a strong foundation in troubleshooting, networking, and customer service. Experienced in diagnosing hardware and software issues, managing Active Directory accounts, and resolving technical problems efficiently. Passionate about providing excellent end-user support and continuously improving technical skills.'

The skills section should list relevant technical competencies, including operating systems, networking, hardware troubleshooting, software applications, and ticketing systems. A well-structured skills section may include:

Operating Systems: Windows, macOS, Linux

Networking: TCP/IP, DNS, DHCP, VPN, firewalls

Software & Tools: Active Directory, Microsoft 365, ServiceNow, Remote Desktop

Security: Multi-Factor Authentication (MFA), endpoint protection, password policies

Scripting: PowerShell, Bash (if applicable)

The work experience section is one of the most important parts of the resume. Each job entry should include the company name, job title, employment dates, and bullet points detailing responsibilities and achievements. Instead of listing generic duties, focusing on quantifiable accomplishments makes a resume stand out. Examples of strong resume bullet points include:

Resolved an average of 50+ support tickets per week, improving first-time resolution rates by 30%.

Assisted in deploying 200+ company laptops during a hardware refresh project, ensuring minimal downtime for employees.

Implemented an updated knowledge base system, reducing repeat tickets by 15% through improved self-service documentation.

For professionals with limited experience, including internships, freelance work, or volunteer IT support roles can demonstrate technical ability and problem-solving skills. Adding projects, such as setting up a home lab with virtual machines, troubleshooting a network issue, or scripting an automation tool, can also highlight hands-on experience.

Education and certifications should be listed near the bottom of the resume. If a candidate has CompTIA A+, Network+, Security+, CCNA, Microsoft 365 certifications, or ITIL Foundation, these credentials should be prominently displayed, as they demonstrate industry-standard knowledge and commitment to professional growth.

Including a short section for professional development, such as completed online courses, technical blogs, or participation in IT forums, can further differentiate a candidate. Hiring managers appreciate applicants who continuously improve their skills through self-learning and professional networking.

Once a resume is well-structured, preparing for the interview process is the next step. IT support interviews typically assess technical skills, problem-solving ability, and communication skills. Candidates should expect technical questions, behavioral questions, and real-world troubleshooting scenarios.

Technical questions often cover basic networking, operating systems, hardware troubleshooting, and IT security. Common questions include:

'What steps would you take to troubleshoot a slow network connection?'

'How would you resolve a user's account being locked out in Active Directory?'

'Can you explain the differences between TCP and UDP?'

'How would you respond to a phishing email reported by a user?'

For technical scenarios, interviewers may present a hypothetical support request and ask the candidate to walk through the troubleshooting process. For example, an interviewer might ask:

'A user calls and says they cannot access the internet, but their coworker sitting next to them has no issues. How would you troubleshoot this?'

A strong response would involve logical troubleshooting steps, such as verifying if the issue is isolated to one device, checking for physical connection problems, confirming network settings, testing with another device, and using command-line tools such as ipconfig and ping to diagnose connectivity.

Behavioral questions assess how candidates handle difficult situations, work under pressure, and communicate with non-technical users. Common questions include:

'Tell me about a time you had to deal with a difficult user. How did you handle it?'

'Describe a situation where you had multiple urgent tickets. How did you prioritize them?'

'Have you ever made a mistake in troubleshooting? How did you correct it?'

When answering behavioral questions, using the STAR method (Situation, Task, Action, Result) helps structure responses effectively. For example:

'A user was frustrated because their email wasn't working. I remained calm, actively listened to their concerns, and investigated the issue. I discovered that their email password had expired, so I guided them through resetting it. They were satisfied with the solution, and I documented the issue in the knowledge base to prevent future confusion.'

Soft skills are just as important as technical skills in IT support interviews. Interviewers evaluate a candidate's ability to communicate clearly, explain technical concepts to non-technical users, and remain patient under pressure. Demonstrating strong interpersonal skills during the interview increases the likelihood of being hired.

Before the interview, candidates should research the company, understand its IT infrastructure, and review any technologies mentioned in the job description. Having specific examples of past experience related to the role helps show that the candidate is well-prepared and knowledgeable.

Practicing mock interviews with a friend, mentor, or online interview platform can help build confidence. Recording practice responses and refining answers ensures a smoother delivery during the actual interview.

Dressing appropriately for the interview, whether virtual or in-person, also leaves a positive impression. Even for IT roles with relaxed dress codes, appearing professional demonstrates respect for the process.

At the end of the interview, candidates should prepare thoughtful questions for the interviewer, such as:

'What are the biggest challenges your IT support team faces?'

'What tools and ticketing systems does your helpdesk use?'

'Are there opportunities for career growth within the company?'

Following up with a thank-you email after the interview expresses appreciation and reinforces interest in the position. A short, professional email thanking the interviewer for their time and reiterating enthusiasm for the role can leave a lasting positive impression.

A strong resume and well-prepared interview strategy significantly increase the chances of landing an IT support role. By highlighting relevant experience, showcasing certifications, practicing troubleshooting scenarios, and demonstrating excellent communication skills, candidates can effectively present themselves as valuable assets to any IT team.

Common Helpdesk Interview Questions and Answers

Preparing for a helpdesk interview requires a strong understanding of technical concepts, troubleshooting methodologies, customer service skills, and problem-solving abilities. Employers look for candidates who can communicate effectively, resolve IT issues efficiently, and maintain professionalism under pressure. Helpdesk analysts should be prepared to answer technical questions, behavioral questions, and scenario-based troubleshooting exercises during an interview. Understanding common interview questions and formulating strong responses increases the chances of securing a job in IT support.

A frequent technical question in helpdesk interviews is: 'What steps would you take to troubleshoot a slow internet connection?' This question tests the candidate's knowledge of networking basics and diagnostic tools. A strong response would outline a logical troubleshooting process such as:

'I would first ask the user if other devices on the same network are experiencing issues to determine whether the problem is isolated. Then, I would check if the issue occurs over both Wi-Fi and Ethernet. If using Wi-Fi, I would ensure the user is within range and not experiencing interference. Next, I would verify the network settings, confirm that the correct IP address is assigned, and test the connection using ping or tracert to identify delays. If needed, I would restart the router, check firewall settings, and escalate the issue to the network team if it appears to be an ISP-related problem.'

Another common question is: 'How would you handle a user who is frustrated or upset?' Helpdesk analysts often deal with users who are stressed due to technical problems affecting their work. Employers want to see candidates demonstrate patience, empathy, and conflict resolution skills. A good response would be:

'First, I would actively listen to the user's concerns and acknowledge their frustration. I would assure them that I understand the urgency and that I am here to help. I would then ask clear, concise questions to diagnose the issue while keeping the conversation calm and professional. If necessary, I would provide a time estimate for resolution and offer alternative solutions if an immediate fix is not possible. Keeping the user informed throughout the process and following up after resolution helps build trust and improve customer satisfaction.'

Interviewers often test knowledge of operating systems by asking: 'What are the key differences between Windows and Linux?' Helpdesk analysts must support various operating systems, making it important to understand their distinctions. A well-rounded answer might be:

'Windows is a proprietary operating system developed by Microsoft, known for its user-friendly interface and compatibility with enterprise applications. It primarily uses NTFS for file management and includes tools like Active Directory for centralized user management. Linux, on the other hand, is an open-source operating system with multiple distributions, such as Ubuntu, CentOS, and Red Hat. It is known for its stability, security, and command-line flexibility using Bash. Unlike Windows, Linux file permissions and package management vary by distribution. While Windows is commonly used in corporate environments, Linux is widely used for servers, development, and security applications.'

A critical question related to security is: 'How would you respond if a user reports receiving a suspicious email?' Phishing attacks are a major security concern, and helpdesk analysts must recognize and mitigate them. A solid response could be:

'I would first advise the user not to click any links or download attachments. Then, I would inspect the email headers to verify the sender's authenticity. If the email contains suspicious requests, such as asking for login credentials or financial information, I would report it to the security team for further analysis. If needed, I would help the user change their password and ensure multi-factor authentication (MFA) is enabled. Finally, I would document the incident and, if necessary, educate the user on recognizing phishing attempts to prevent future occurrences.'

Many interviews include a scenario-based troubleshooting question, such as: 'A user's computer won't turn on. What steps would you take to diagnose the issue?' A structured response demonstrating problem-solving skills is important. A good answer would follow a step-by-step diagnostic process:

'First, I would check whether the computer is plugged in and if the power cable and outlet are functional. If there are no external power issues, I would look for any signs of life, such as LED lights or fan noise. If the computer still does not turn on, I would try a different power supply or battery (if it's a laptop). Next, I would check for hardware failures, such as a defective RAM stick or a faulty motherboard. If necessary, I would escalate the issue to the hardware support team for further investigation.'

Employers also assess knowledge of IT support tools by asking: 'What is a ticketing system, and why is it important?' Helpdesk analysts rely on ticketing systems to track, prioritize, and resolve user requests efficiently. A strong response would include:

'A ticketing system is a software application used to log, manage, and track IT support requests. It allows IT teams to prioritize issues, document troubleshooting steps, and ensure timely resolutions. Ticketing systems help improve efficiency by categorizing incidents, automating workflows, and providing historical data for recurring problems. Examples of ticketing systems include ServiceNow, Zendesk, and Jira Service Management. Using a structured system ensures accountability and improves the overall user support experience.'

Another question that frequently arises is: 'How would you handle a situation where you do not know the answer to a technical problem?' IT professionals often encounter unfamiliar issues, and interviewers want to see problem-solving skills and adaptability. A good response would be:

'If I do not know the answer, I would first attempt to research the issue using internal documentation, knowledge bases, and online resources. If I still need assistance, I would consult a colleague or escalate the issue to a higher-level support team. I would ensure that I document the resolution once the issue is solved so that I can handle similar problems in the future. The key is to remain calm, resourceful, and proactive in finding a solution rather than guessing.´

Helpdesk analysts should also be prepared for behavioral questions such as: ´Tell me about a time when you had to multitask under pressure.´ Employers want to assess how well candidates handle high workloads and prioritize tasks. A response using the STAR method (Situation, Task, Action, Result) would be effective:

´During a major software rollout, I was handling multiple user requests while troubleshooting an unexpected system issue. I prioritized critical tickets affecting system functionality while guiding other users to self-service resources. By staying organized, using time management strategies, and collaborating with my team, we successfully resolved all issues within the service-level agreement timeframe.´

To prepare for a helpdesk interview, candidates should study common IT issues, review technical concepts, and practice troubleshooting scenarios. Strong communication skills, a structured problem-solving approach, and a customer-focused mindset are key factors in impressing interviewers. By demonstrating technical expertise, adaptability, and professionalism, candidates can confidently navigate IT support interviews and secure their desired roles.

Understanding IT Compliance and Regulations

IT compliance and regulations play a critical role in ensuring that organizations protect sensitive data, maintain security, and adhere to legal and industry standards. Compliance refers to the process of following laws, policies, and frameworks that govern how data is stored, processed, and accessed. Failure to comply with these regulations can lead to financial penalties, legal consequences, and reputational damage. Helpdesk analysts, while not directly responsible for regulatory compliance, must understand the fundamental principles of IT compliance and how their daily tasks contribute to maintaining a secure and compliant environment.

One of the most well-known regulations in IT security is the General Data Protection Regulation (GDPR), which applies to any organization handling the personal data of European Union (EU) citizens. GDPR mandates strict data protection measures, including user consent, data encryption, access controls, and breach notification requirements. Organizations must ensure that personal data is collected lawfully and stored securely. Helpdesk analysts play a role in enforcing security policies, managing user access, and assisting with data protection measures to help organizations remain GDPR compliant.

In the healthcare industry, the Health Insurance Portability and Accountability Act (HIPAA) establishes standards for protecting patient information in the United States. HIPAA requires healthcare providers and business associates to safeguard electronic health records (EHRs) from unauthorized access, breaches, or misuse. IT teams must implement access controls, encryption, and secure authentication methods to protect patient data. Helpdesk analysts working in healthcare IT must ensure that employees follow security protocols when accessing patient information and report any suspicious activity that could lead to a HIPAA violation.

For organizations handling payment card transactions, the Payment Card Industry Data Security Standard (PCI DSS) establishes strict guidelines for protecting credit card data. PCI DSS compliance involves encrypting payment data, restricting access to cardholder information, maintaining secure networks, and conducting regular security assessments. Helpdesk analysts must follow best practices, such as ensuring workstations processing payments are secure, monitoring for unauthorized access, and educating employees on safe payment handling procedures. Organizations that fail to comply with PCI DSS can face severe financial penalties and restrictions from payment processing providers.

The finance sector is governed by the Sarbanes-Oxley Act (SOX), which was enacted to prevent corporate fraud and ensure accurate financial reporting. SOX compliance requires companies to implement IT controls, audit trails, and cybersecurity measures to protect financial data. IT teams must monitor system logs, enforce authentication policies, and ensure that financial data is not altered or accessed by unauthorized users. Helpdesk analysts play a role in SOX compliance by maintaining secure access to financial systems, managing user permissions, and responding to security alerts.

Another important compliance framework is ISO/IEC 27001, which is an international standard for information security management. ISO 27001 provides guidelines for establishing risk management strategies, implementing security controls, and continuously improving an organization's security posture. Organizations that achieve ISO 27001 certification demonstrate a strong commitment to protecting sensitive information. Helpdesk analysts contribute to compliance by following security policies, applying software updates, and educating users on cybersecurity best practices.

The United States government enforces the Federal Information Security Management Act (FISMA), which requires federal agencies to implement risk-based security controls to protect government data. IT teams working in government or defense-related industries must ensure compliance with National Institute of Standards and Technology (NIST) cybersecurity frameworks, which outline security best practices for protecting government networks and infrastructure. Helpdesk analysts supporting federal agencies must follow strict security protocols, including identity verification, secure remote access procedures, and encryption requirements.

For cloud computing and online services, the Cloud Security Alliance (CSA) and SOC 2 (Service Organization Control 2) compliance frameworks establish security guidelines for data protection, privacy, and vendor management. SOC 2 compliance ensures that cloud providers follow strict security, availability, and confidentiality standards. Helpdesk analysts working for cloud-based organizations must assist in securing cloud accounts, monitoring access logs, and implementing multi-factor authentication (MFA) to help maintain compliance.

Compliance is not just about following regulations—it also involves security awareness training and risk management. Many compliance frameworks require organizations to educate employees on security policies, phishing awareness, and data protection best practices. Helpdesk analysts are often the first line of defense in IT security, as they interact directly with users who may be unaware of security threats. Educating users on password management, phishing detection, and device security helps reduce compliance risks.

Organizations must also conduct regular security audits and assessments to identify vulnerabilities and ensure compliance with regulations. Audits typically include penetration testing, vulnerability scans, access control reviews, and data encryption verification. Helpdesk analysts assist in compliance audits by providing system logs, ensuring that software patches are applied, and documenting security incidents.

Incident response is another critical aspect of IT compliance. Many regulations require organizations to have a data breach response plan, outlining how to detect, report, and mitigate security incidents. For example, GDPR requires organizations to notify authorities within 72 hours of discovering a data breach. Helpdesk analysts play a role in incident response by escalating security incidents, containing threats, and assisting users affected by breaches.

Data retention and disposal policies are also governed by compliance regulations. Many laws specify how long data must be retained, when it should be deleted, and how it must be securely disposed of. For example, financial records under SOX must be retained for at least seven years, while HIPAA mandates that medical records be stored securely for a specific period depending on state laws. IT teams must ensure that obsolete data is properly deleted or encrypted to prevent unauthorized access.

Compliance requirements also extend to third-party vendors and service providers. Organizations must ensure that their partners adhere to the same security and regulatory standards. For example, businesses that use cloud storage providers must verify that those providers comply with GDPR, SOC 2, or ISO 27001 standards. Helpdesk analysts may be involved in assisting vendors with secure access to company systems and verifying compliance documentation.

To stay compliant with evolving regulations, organizations must continuously update their security policies and IT infrastructure. Governments and regulatory bodies frequently introduce new laws and amendments in response to emerging cybersecurity threats. IT teams must remain proactive by monitoring compliance updates, implementing security improvements, and conducting periodic training sessions.

Understanding IT compliance and regulations is essential for maintaining data security, reducing legal risks, and protecting an organization's reputation. Helpdesk analysts contribute to compliance by following security policies, educating users, assisting in audits, and supporting incident response efforts. By staying informed about regulations such as GDPR, HIPAA, PCI DSS, SOX, and ISO 27001, IT professionals help ensure that their organizations operate securely and in accordance with industry standards.

Supporting End Users in Different Work Environments (Office, Hybrid, Remote)

The modern workplace has evolved significantly, with employees working in traditional office environments, hybrid setups, and fully remote locations. Each work environment presents unique challenges for IT support teams, requiring helpdesk analysts to adapt their troubleshooting methods, security protocols, and communication strategies to ensure seamless productivity. Supporting end users in these diverse settings demands a flexible approach, robust IT infrastructure, and an emphasis on security and user experience.

In a traditional office environment, IT support teams have direct access to user devices, networks, and on-site infrastructure. Analysts can physically inspect workstations, troubleshoot hardware issues, and provide face-to-face assistance. Office environments typically have centralized networks, making it easier to enforce security policies, software updates, and access controls. Employees connect to corporate Wi-Fi and internal servers, allowing IT teams to manage assets through Active Directory (AD), group policies, and on-premise helpdesk systems.

Common issues in office environments include network connectivity problems, printer malfunctions, software crashes, and hardware failures. Since IT staff are physically present, troubleshooting these issues is often more straightforward. Helpdesk analysts can quickly check network cables, swap out defective peripherals, and reinstall software without remote limitations. Office setups also benefit from dedicated IT support desks, where employees can bring devices for troubleshooting or receive hands-on training for new software and policies.

However, hybrid work environments introduce a mix of office-based and remote employees, creating new challenges for IT teams. Hybrid setups require secure remote access solutions, seamless collaboration tools, and consistent user experiences across multiple locations. Employees may work some days in the office and others from home, meaning IT support must manage devices across different networks, troubleshoot remote connectivity issues, and ensure data security outside the corporate perimeter.

One of the most critical aspects of hybrid support is Virtual Private Network (VPN) access. Employees working from home must securely connect to corporate resources, such as internal file shares, intranet applications, and cloud services. VPN issues, including slow connections, dropped sessions, or authentication failures, are common helpdesk tickets in hybrid work environments. Analysts must ensure that users have the correct VPN client installed, their credentials are valid, and their network settings allow for stable connectivity.

Collaboration tools like Microsoft Teams, Zoom, Google Meet, and Slack are essential for hybrid workers. IT teams must troubleshoot audio/video problems, resolve login issues, and manage access to virtual meetings. Many hybrid employees also require cloud storage solutions, such as OneDrive, Google Drive, or Dropbox, to access files from multiple locations. Ensuring proper file synchronization, access permissions, and data encryption is crucial for productivity and security.

Device management becomes more complex in hybrid settings, as employees frequently move between locations. IT teams must deploy Mobile Device Management (MDM) solutions, such as Microsoft Intune or VMware Workspace ONE, to monitor, update, and secure company-issued laptops, tablets, and smartphones. MDM policies help enforce encryption, password policies, and remote wipe capabilities in case a device is lost or stolen.

Fully remote work environments present the most significant challenges for IT support, as users operate from various locations, networks, and devices. Unlike office-based employees, remote workers do not have direct access to corporate IT infrastructure, meaning all troubleshooting must be handled via remote support tools. Analysts rely on remote desktop applications like TeamViewer, AnyDesk, LogMeIn, or Microsoft Remote Desktop Protocol (RDP) to diagnose and resolve issues.

One of the most frequent remote work issues is home network instability. Users may experience slow internet speeds, weak Wi-Fi signals, or connectivity drops, which can impact productivity, especially during virtual meetings. Helpdesk analysts must guide users through network diagnostics, such as rebooting routers, using Ethernet instead of Wi-Fi, and identifying bandwidth-heavy applications that may be causing slow speeds.

Security is a major concern in remote environments. Employees working from home may use personal devices, unsecured networks, or weak passwords, increasing the risk of cyber threats. IT teams must enforce Multi-Factor Authentication (MFA), endpoint security software, and strict access controls to protect corporate data. Analysts should educate remote employees on phishing awareness, safe browsing habits, and the importance of regular software updates.

Remote workers often face hardware-related issues, such as failing laptop batteries, overheating devices, or unresponsive peripherals. Unlike office environments, where IT staff can physically replace faulty components, remote users must rely on self-troubleshooting guides or shipment of replacement hardware. Helpdesk teams should maintain detailed troubleshooting documentation and offer guided support sessions to help users resolve common hardware issues.

Another challenge in remote support is time zone differences. Large organizations with globally distributed teams require IT support to accommodate employees working in different time zones. Some companies implement follow-the-sun support models, ensuring 24/7 helpdesk coverage across different regions. IT teams may also set up self-service portals and AI-powered chatbots to provide assistance outside standard business hours.

Ensuring consistent security policies across office, hybrid, and remote environments requires Zero Trust Architecture (ZTA). Zero Trust enforces strict identity verification, continuous monitoring, and least-privilege access principles regardless of a user's location. IT teams use identity and access management (IAM) solutions, such as Okta, Microsoft Entra ID (formerly Azure AD), or Google Workspace IAM, to ensure that users only have access to the systems and data necessary for their roles.

To provide effective support in all work environments, IT teams should regularly update documentation, conduct user training, and refine troubleshooting workflows. Employees should have access to step-by-step guides, video tutorials, and FAQs to resolve minor issues independently. Training sessions on best practices for remote security, software usage, and collaboration tools can significantly reduce the volume of helpdesk tickets.

Proactive IT management is essential for preventing issues before they disrupt work. Implementing automated monitoring systems helps detect and resolve problems before users report them. For example, IT teams can use remote monitoring and management (RMM) tools to track device health, software updates, and network performance across all user locations.

Effective communication is key when supporting diverse work environments. IT support teams should maintain clear channels for reporting issues, tracking ticket progress, and providing real-time updates on system outages or maintenance schedules. Using internal chat platforms, email alerts, and helpdesk dashboards, analysts can keep employees informed and minimize disruptions.

By adapting to the unique challenges of office, hybrid, and remote work environments, helpdesk analysts ensure seamless IT support, enhanced productivity, and strong security practices. Whether troubleshooting in-person, guiding remote users, or managing hybrid setups, IT professionals must remain proactive, adaptable, and security-focused to support modern workplaces effectively.

How to Provide Training and IT Guidance to Users

Providing IT training and guidance to users is a crucial responsibility for helpdesk analysts. Many technical issues arise due to a lack of understanding of systems, security policies, and best practices. By equipping users with the knowledge and skills to handle basic IT tasks independently, organizations can reduce the volume of support tickets, enhance cybersecurity awareness, and improve overall productivity. Effective IT training requires clear communication, patience, and an ability to adapt teaching methods to different learning styles.

One of the first steps in delivering IT training is assessing the knowledge level of users. Employees come from diverse backgrounds, and their familiarity with technology varies widely. Some users may be highly proficient with software applications and troubleshooting, while others may struggle with basic IT tasks, such as managing emails or using collaboration tools. Conducting a pre-training assessment, surveys, or one-on-one discussions helps IT teams tailor their training sessions to the needs of specific user groups.

Training sessions should be structured with a clear agenda and learning objectives. Users are more engaged when they understand why the training is necessary and how it will benefit them. Whether the session covers cybersecurity awareness, new software implementation, or troubleshooting common IT issues, outlining the key topics at the beginning ensures that employees know what to expect. Providing real-world examples, interactive demonstrations, and hands-on exercises reinforces learning and helps users retain information more effectively.

IT guidance can be delivered through various training formats, including in-person workshops, virtual training sessions, self-paced online courses, video tutorials, and step-by-step guides. Choosing the right format depends on the complexity of the topic, the availability of users, and the resources of the IT department.

In-person workshops are ideal for hands-on training sessions where users need direct interaction with IT instructors. These sessions work well for teaching employees how to use new hardware, software, or security tools. In-person training allows users to ask questions in real-time, practice on their devices, and receive immediate assistance with troubleshooting. However, scheduling and logistics can be a challenge, especially in organizations with remote or hybrid employees.

Virtual training sessions conducted via Microsoft Teams, Zoom, or Google Meet provide a flexible alternative for organizations with dispersed workforces. These sessions can be recorded and shared with employees who cannot attend live, allowing them to revisit the material at their convenience. Virtual training should incorporate screen-sharing, live demonstrations, and Q&A segments to keep users engaged. IT trainers should encourage participants to enable their cameras, participate in discussions, and practice the tasks being taught to ensure a more interactive experience.

Self-paced learning resources, such as knowledge base articles, FAQ sections, and video tutorials, allow users to learn at their own speed. A well-maintained knowledge base reduces the number of repetitive IT support requests by providing step-by-step guides for common tasks, such as resetting passwords, configuring email clients, and troubleshooting network connectivity. IT teams should regularly update and expand the knowledge base to ensure that it remains relevant and helpful.

IT training should also include a strong emphasis on cybersecurity awareness. Many security breaches occur due to human error, such as falling for phishing emails, using weak passwords, or downloading unverified applications. Helpdesk analysts should educate users on recognizing social engineering attacks, securing their devices, and following company security policies. Providing real-life phishing simulations, password management best practices, and guidance on safe browsing habits helps employees develop a security-first mindset.

Encouraging hands-on learning improves user retention. Instead of lecturing users about software features or troubleshooting steps, IT trainers should guide them through interactive exercises where they perform the tasks themselves. For example, if training employees on using a new cloud storage solution, the trainer should instruct them to upload, share, and organize files during the session rather than just demonstrating the process.

Technical training should be customized to different user roles and responsibilities. Employees in finance, HR, marketing, and IT departments use technology in different ways and require specialized guidance. IT teams should develop role-based training programs that focus on the specific applications, security concerns, and troubleshooting needs relevant to each department.

Reinforcing training through ongoing support and follow-ups ensures that users retain what they have learned. IT teams should schedule refresher courses, provide updates on new technology changes, and be available for follow-up questions. Many users may struggle to apply their training in real-world scenarios, so having an IT mentor program, office hours, or a dedicated support channel helps users feel supported even after the initial training.

Measuring the effectiveness of IT training is essential for continuous improvement. IT teams should collect feedback through post-training surveys, quizzes, or practical assessments to gauge how well users understood the material. If multiple employees still struggle with a particular task or concept, the training content may need to be refined, simplified, or reinforced with additional resources.

IT teams should also focus on making training accessible and user-friendly. Avoiding excessive technical jargon, breaking down complex concepts into easy-to-follow steps, and providing visual aids such as diagrams and screenshots improve comprehension. Encouraging a friendly, non-judgmental learning environment makes users more comfortable asking questions and seeking help.

Incorporating gamification elements into training can boost engagement. Quizzes, reward systems, and competition-based learning encourage employees to actively participate in training.

Organizations can implement IT knowledge challenges, security awareness competitions, or badge-based achievement systems to keep employees motivated to expand their technical skills.

Promoting a culture of continuous learning ensures that IT knowledge remains up to date. The IT landscape is constantly evolving, with new software updates, security threats, and productivity tools emerging regularly. Encouraging employees to stay informed about IT best practices, explore new features of the tools they use, and seek IT training proactively helps create a more tech-savvy workforce.

Providing IT training and guidance to users is not just about fixing problems as they arise, but about empowering employees with the knowledge and confidence to use technology effectively. When users understand how to troubleshoot minor issues, follow security best practices, and utilize IT tools efficiently, the organization benefits from fewer support requests, improved security, and increased productivity. IT professionals must continually refine their training methods, adapt to user needs, and foster a proactive learning environment to enhance the overall IT experience within the organization.

Staying Updated with the Latest IT Trends and Technologies

The field of information technology is constantly evolving, with new advancements in cloud computing, cybersecurity, artificial intelligence, automation, and networking emerging every year. Helpdesk analysts must stay informed about these developments to remain effective in their roles and continue advancing in their careers. Failing to keep up with the latest IT trends can result in outdated knowledge, inefficient troubleshooting, and a lack of preparedness for new security threats. Developing a habit of continuous learning ensures that IT professionals remain competitive, capable, and valuable in an ever-changing industry.

One of the most effective ways to stay updated with IT trends is by following reputable tech news sources and industry blogs. Websites such as TechCrunch, Ars Technica, Wired, The Verge, and ZDNet provide daily updates on the latest developments in hardware, software, and enterprise technology. Cybersecurity-focused sources like Krebs on Security, Dark Reading, and the SANS Internet Storm Center help IT professionals stay informed about new security vulnerabilities, data breaches, and malware threats. Regularly reading these publications provides insights into emerging technologies, regulatory changes, and IT best practices.

Subscribing to IT newsletters and RSS feeds is another effective way to receive updates directly. Many leading tech companies and security organizations send weekly or monthly newsletters summarizing the most important industry news. Subscribing to sources such as Microsoft's Tech Community, Google Cloud Blog, AWS News, and Cisco Blogs keeps IT professionals informed about the latest software updates, patches, and best practices.

Attending technology conferences, webinars, and industry events is a valuable way to gain hands-on experience with new technologies. Conferences like CES, Black Hat, DEF CON, Microsoft Ignite, Google Cloud Next, and AWS re:Invent showcase the latest innovations in AI, cloud computing, security, and automation. These events often feature live demos, panel discussions, and keynote speeches from industry leaders. Even if attending in person is not possible, many conferences offer free virtual sessions or post their content online for later viewing.

Engaging with IT communities and discussion forums provides opportunities to learn from peers and share knowledge. Platforms like Reddit's r/sysadmin, r/techsupport, and r/cybersecurity, as well as Stack Exchange and Spiceworks, allow IT professionals to discuss troubleshooting techniques, new technologies, and industry challenges. Participating in these communities helps analysts gain real-world insights from others who have encountered similar technical issues or adopted new tools.

Social media is another powerful tool for staying updated. Following industry experts, technology companies, and security researchers on LinkedIn, Twitter, and YouTube provides direct access to breaking news and professional discussions. Many experts share technical deep dives, vulnerability reports, and best practices that are not always covered in traditional media. Watching IT-related YouTube channels such as NetworkChuck, Linus Tech Tips, and Cybersecurity Meg can provide both in-depth tutorials and high-level overviews of emerging trends.

Earning IT certifications and enrolling in online courses ensures that professionals keep their skills relevant. Platforms such as Pluralsight, Udemy, Coursera, and LinkedIn Learning offer courses on cloud computing, networking, cybersecurity, DevOps, and automation. Certification programs from CompTIA, Cisco, Microsoft, AWS, and Google Cloud provide structured learning paths that align with industry demands. Some of the most valuable certifications for helpdesk analysts looking to expand their knowledge include CompTIA Security+, AWS Certified Cloud Practitioner, Microsoft Azure Fundamentals, and Cisco CCNA.

Practicing hands-on learning in a home lab is one of the best ways to develop technical expertise. Setting up virtual environments using VMware, VirtualBox, or Hyper-V allows IT professionals to experiment with Linux distributions, Windows Server configurations, Active Directory, and cloud services without the risk of disrupting production systems. Building a test network, simulating security attacks in a controlled environment, or scripting automation tasks with PowerShell, Python, or Bash helps reinforce theoretical knowledge with practical experience.

Experimenting with open-source tools and technologies broadens technical skills. Many industry-standard applications, such as Wireshark for network analysis, Metasploit for penetration testing, and Docker for containerization, are freely available for testing and learning. Exploring these tools helps analysts develop new troubleshooting techniques and gain insights into how modern IT infrastructure is managed and secured.

Cybersecurity is a rapidly evolving field, making it essential for helpdesk analysts to stay ahead of new attack vectors, social engineering tactics, and malware developments. Organizations like CISA, NIST, and the Center for Internet Security (CIS) regularly publish security advisories and best practices for protecting IT environments. Keeping up with Common Vulnerabilities and

Exposures (CVE) reports helps IT professionals understand which security threats require immediate attention.

Automation and scripting are becoming increasingly important in IT support roles. Learning how to automate repetitive tasks using PowerShell, Python, or Bash can significantly improve efficiency and reduce manual errors. Many IT departments use Ansible, Terraform, or Puppet to manage infrastructure as code, and understanding these tools can open opportunities for career advancement into DevOps and system administration.

AI and machine learning are transforming IT support, with AI-driven chatbots, predictive analytics, and intelligent automation being integrated into helpdesk environments. Platforms like Microsoft Copilot, ChatGPT for IT support, and Google AI-powered analytics are changing how IT teams handle troubleshooting and user requests. Understanding how these technologies work and how to integrate them into daily IT operations ensures that helpdesk analysts stay relevant as automation plays a larger role in technical support.

Cloud computing continues to reshape IT infrastructure, making it essential for IT professionals to familiarize themselves with platforms like Amazon Web Services (AWS), Microsoft Azure, and Google Cloud Platform (GCP). Many companies are shifting from on-premise servers to hybrid or fully cloud-based solutions, requiring IT teams to support cloud-hosted applications, storage, and virtual desktops. Gaining hands-on experience with cloud-based identity management, storage solutions, and serverless computing positions IT professionals for higher-level technical roles.

Helpdesk analysts should also pay attention to emerging workplace technologies, such as virtual desktop infrastructure (VDI), zero trust security models, and endpoint detection and response (EDR) solutions. As remote work and hybrid environments become more common, IT teams must adapt to new security challenges and support structures. Learning how to manage remote access, cloud-based authentication, and collaboration tools ensures that analysts can support users in modern work environments.

Staying updated with IT trends requires curiosity, adaptability, and a proactive approach to learning. By regularly consuming tech news, participating in industry discussions, experimenting with new tools, and obtaining certifications, IT professionals can keep their skills sharp and remain valuable in the ever-changing technology landscape. Helpdesk analysts who embrace continuous learning position themselves for career growth, specialized roles, and leadership opportunities in IT.

Creating a Personal Development Plan for Career Progression

Developing a structured personal development plan (PDP) is essential for career progression in the IT industry. A PDP provides a clear roadmap for acquiring new skills, achieving professional milestones, and advancing into higher-level roles. Without a plan, career growth can become stagnant, leading to missed opportunities and lack of motivation. Helpdesk analysts who create and follow a well-defined PDP can transition into specialized roles such as system administration, cybersecurity, cloud computing, networking, or IT management. Establishing a structured plan helps individuals identify goals, set timelines, track progress, and stay accountable.

The first step in creating a personal development plan is to assess current skills and experience. Conducting a self-evaluation helps determine strengths, weaknesses, and areas for improvement. Helpdesk analysts should analyze their technical skills, troubleshooting abilities, communication effectiveness, and leadership potential. Identifying knowledge gaps makes it easier to prioritize which skills need development and which strengths can be leveraged for career advancement.

Setting clear and measurable career goals is the next critical step. Goals should be specific, achievable, and aligned with long-term career aspirations. For example, instead of setting a vague goal like 'I want to improve my networking skills,' a more effective goal would be 'I will earn the CompTIA Network+ certification within the next six months to strengthen my understanding of network troubleshooting and prepare for a network engineer role.´ Using the SMART (Specific, Measurable, Achievable, Relevant, Time-bound) framework ensures that goals remain realistic and trackable.

Once goals are defined, the next step is researching the skills and certifications required to reach the desired career position. Each IT specialization has specific skill requirements. For example:

System Administrators need expertise in Windows Server, Linux, Active Directory, and virtualization.

Cybersecurity Analysts require knowledge of firewalls, penetration testing, incident response, and security frameworks like NIST and CIS.

Cloud Engineers must understand AWS, Microsoft Azure, Google Cloud, containerization, and automation.

Network Engineers should master Cisco networking, routing and switching, VLANs, and network security.

Identifying which certifications align with career goals helps structure a learning path. Some common certifications include CompTIA A+, Network+, Security+, Cisco CCNA, Microsoft Azure Fundamentals, AWS Certified Solutions Architect, and Certified Ethical Hacker (CEH). Enrolling in training courses, watching tutorials, and practicing in a home lab environment builds hands-on experience and increases technical confidence.

Developing soft skills is equally important for career progression. IT professionals must be effective communicators, problem solvers, and team players. Helpdesk analysts who aspire to leadership roles should focus on building leadership, project management, and customer service skills. Participating in team projects, mentoring junior colleagues, and leading small initiatives strengthens leadership capabilities.

Time management is critical when working on personal development. Balancing full-time work, certification studies, and skill-building exercises requires effective scheduling and discipline. Setting aside dedicated study hours each week, breaking down learning objectives into smaller tasks, and tracking progress using productivity tools like Trello, Notion, or Microsoft Planner ensures steady advancement.

Seeking mentorship and networking opportunities accelerates career growth. Connecting with experienced IT professionals through LinkedIn, industry events, and online communities provides valuable insights, career guidance, and potential job opportunities. Many IT professionals are willing to mentor individuals who show enthusiasm and dedication. Participating in technology forums, attending meetups, and engaging in discussions with industry experts expands knowledge and fosters professional relationships.

Hands-on practice is crucial for mastering new technologies. Setting up a home lab using VirtualBox, VMware, or cloud-based virtual machines allows IT professionals to experiment with server configurations, networking setups, security tools, and automation scripts. Practical experience strengthens troubleshooting skills, builds technical confidence, and enhances resume qualifications.

Regularly updating and refining the personal development plan ensures continuous progress. As new technologies emerge and industry demands evolve, IT professionals must adapt their learning paths, update their goals, and refine their skill sets. Reviewing progress every three to six months helps assess what has been achieved and what adjustments need to be made.

Documenting achievements and milestones is essential for career advancement and job applications. Keeping a portfolio of completed projects, earned certifications, and technical skills provides concrete proof of expertise. Maintaining an updated resume and LinkedIn profile showcasing accomplishments makes it easier to apply for new roles and negotiate promotions.

Applying new skills in a professional setting reinforces learning. Volunteering for new IT projects, assisting with system upgrades, troubleshooting complex issues, and taking initiative allows helpdesk analysts to gain practical experience beyond their routine responsibilities. Demonstrating technical expertise, problem-solving abilities, and leadership potential increases visibility within an organization and creates opportunities for promotions.

For those aiming for higher-level positions, learning about business and IT alignment is crucial. Understanding how IT supports business objectives, contributes to operational efficiency, and enhances security compliance makes IT professionals more valuable to employers. Enrolling in courses related to IT project management, ITIL service management, and business process improvement expands career prospects.

Staying motivated and overcoming challenges is an essential part of career progression. Learning new technologies can be overwhelming and time-consuming, but staying consistent and celebrating small achievements helps maintain motivation. Connecting with like-minded professionals who are also pursuing career growth creates a support system for knowledge-sharing and encouragement.

Creating a personal development plan ensures that IT professionals remain focused, goal-oriented, and continuously improving. By following a structured roadmap that includes self-assessment, goal-setting, skills development, networking, mentorship, and hands-on practice, helpdesk analysts can transition into more advanced roles and establish long-term career success.

Freelancing and Remote Helpdesk Opportunities

The IT support industry has evolved significantly with the rise of freelancing and remote work. Traditional helpdesk roles that once required employees to be physically present in an office are now increasingly available as remote or freelance positions, allowing IT professionals to work from anywhere in the world. Advancements in cloud-based support tools, remote access software, and global collaboration platforms have made it easier than ever for helpdesk analysts to provide technical assistance without being on-site. Many businesses now outsource IT support to freelancers, managed service providers (MSPs), or remote helpdesk teams, creating new opportunities for IT professionals who want to work independently or from home.

Freelancing in IT support allows professionals to offer technical services on a contract or project basis rather than working as full-time employees. Freelancers typically find work through online job platforms, networking, or referrals. Websites such as Upwork, Fiverr, Freelancer, and PeoplePerHour connect IT professionals with businesses and individuals who need remote troubleshooting, network setup, cybersecurity consulting, software installation, and general technical support. Many small businesses, startups, and even large corporations prefer hiring freelancers for short-term or specialized IT needs instead of maintaining a full-time in-house support team.

One of the main advantages of freelancing is the flexibility to choose clients, projects, and work schedules. Freelancers have the freedom to set their own rates, negotiate contracts, and specialize in specific areas of IT support. Some professionals focus on Windows or macOS troubleshooting, while others offer expertise in network security, cloud support, or enterprise software solutions. Specializing in high-demand areas such as Microsoft 365 administration, cybersecurity best practices, or VoIP troubleshooting can make a freelancer more competitive in the marketplace.

Remote helpdesk jobs are another growing opportunity for IT professionals. Many companies, including tech startups, SaaS providers, and MSPs, employ remote IT support specialists to handle ticketing systems, software troubleshooting, and user support requests. Remote helpdesk roles often require strong communication skills, the ability to diagnose issues efficiently, and familiarity with common IT support tools such as ServiceNow, Zendesk, Freshdesk, or SolarWinds. Analysts working remotely must also be self-disciplined, organized, and proactive in managing their workload since they do not have direct supervision in an office environment.

To succeed in freelancing or remote IT support, professionals must have the right tools and software to manage their work efficiently. Essential tools include remote access software (TeamViewer, AnyDesk, LogMeIn), cloud-based ticketing systems, and secure communication platforms (Slack, Microsoft Teams, Zoom). Many IT freelancers also use virtual private networks (VPNs) and endpoint security software to ensure secure connections when working with clients' systems.

Building a strong online presence is critical for securing freelancing opportunities. Many IT freelancers create professional profiles on LinkedIn, GitHub, or personal websites showcasing their expertise, certifications, and past work experience. Publishing IT-related blog posts, troubleshooting guides, or video tutorials on platforms like YouTube or Medium can also help establish credibility and attract potential clients. Many successful freelancers market themselves by offering free initial consultations, responding quickly to job postings, and building relationships with repeat clients.

Pricing services effectively is another important aspect of freelancing. Rates for IT support services vary depending on experience, specialization, project complexity, and client location. Freelancers typically charge by hourly rate, fixed project fee, or monthly retainer for ongoing support. Beginners may start with lower rates to gain experience and build a portfolio, but experienced IT professionals can charge premium rates for specialized or high-level technical support. Many freelancers use value-based pricing, where they charge based on the business impact of the service provided rather than just the time spent on a task.

Freelancing and remote work also require effective time management and productivity skills. Since IT support can involve handling multiple clients or tickets simultaneously, prioritizing urgent issues, setting clear work boundaries, and using task management tools are essential. Many remote IT professionals use Trello, Asana, or Microsoft Planner to track tasks and deadlines. Automating repetitive tasks with scripts, chatbots, or self-service knowledge bases can also improve efficiency and reduce workload.

One challenge of freelancing is client communication and expectation management. IT freelancers must ensure clear communication regarding service scope, response times, and pricing to avoid misunderstandings. Writing detailed proposals, setting service level agreements (SLAs), and maintaining professional customer service helps build trust and secure long-term clients. Regular follow-ups, status updates, and documentation of support sessions demonstrate reliability and improve client satisfaction.

Another challenge of freelancing is ensuring consistent income. Unlike full-time employment, freelance work may have fluctuating workloads and payment delays. Many freelancers diversify their income streams by offering multiple services, working with several clients simultaneously, or providing ongoing support contracts. Some IT professionals combine freelancing with part-time remote jobs, online training courses, or affiliate marketing for tech-related products to stabilize their income.

Freelancers and remote IT professionals must also stay updated with industry trends and certifications to remain competitive. Earning relevant certifications, such as CompTIA A+, Network+, Security+, Microsoft 365 Certified, AWS Certified Cloud Practitioner, or Cisco CCNA, enhances credibility and increases earning potential. Continuous learning through online courses, webinars, and IT community forums ensures that IT professionals stay ahead of emerging technologies, security threats, and evolving best practices.

Cybersecurity is a key concern for freelancers and remote helpdesk analysts. Working from home or accessing client systems remotely introduces security risks, including phishing attacks, data breaches, and unauthorized access. IT freelancers should implement multi-factor authentication (MFA), encrypted communications, and secure password management to protect sensitive information. Using separate business accounts, securing personal devices, and avoiding public Wi-Fi networks further reduces security risks.

Despite its challenges, freelancing and remote helpdesk work offer significant career opportunities, financial independence, and work-life balance. Many IT professionals choose freelancing as a way to transition into specialized IT consulting, build their own businesses, or gain international work experience. Remote IT support also provides opportunities to work with global clients, expanding career prospects beyond local job markets.

Freelancing and remote IT support roles empower IT professionals to take control of their careers, choose projects that match their interests, and build diverse technical expertise. Whether working as an independent contractor, part of a remote support team, or offering specialized IT consulting services, these career paths provide flexibility, growth potential, and financial rewards for those who are proactive, adaptable, and committed to continuous learning.

Transitioning from Helpdesk to Other IT Roles

Working in a helpdesk or service desk role provides a strong foundation for advancing into other IT positions. Many professionals begin their IT careers in technical support and later move into specialized fields such as network administration, system administration, cybersecurity, cloud computing, software development, DevOps, or IT management. Transitioning from helpdesk to another IT role requires continuous skill development, hands-on experience, certifications, and strategic career planning. By taking the right steps, helpdesk analysts can position themselves for long-term success in the IT industry.

One of the most important steps in transitioning to a new role is identifying career interests and goals. IT is a vast field with many specialties, and each requires different skills and knowledge. Some helpdesk professionals prefer working with hardware and networking, making a career in network administration or system administration a natural fit. Others may enjoy security, scripting, or automation, leading them toward cybersecurity, DevOps, or cloud computing. Understanding which aspects of IT are most engaging helps professionals focus their learning efforts and pursue relevant career paths.

Developing technical skills beyond basic troubleshooting is essential for career advancement. Helpdesk roles provide exposure to common IT support tools, operating systems, networking concepts, and ticketing systems, but transitioning to a specialized field requires deeper technical expertise. For example, moving into network administration requires knowledge of TCP/IP, subnetting, VLANs,

178

routers, firewalls, and Cisco networking technologies. A helpdesk analyst interested in system administration should gain experience with Windows Server, Linux, virtualization, and Active Directory management. Those looking to enter cybersecurity must develop skills in penetration testing, threat analysis, and security frameworks like NIST and CIS.

Earning industry-recognized certifications is one of the best ways to demonstrate expertise and qualify for advanced roles. Certifications validate technical knowledge and show employers that candidates have the necessary skills for specialized IT positions. Some of the most valuable certifications for transitioning out of helpdesk include:

CompTIA Network+ – Foundational networking certification for roles in network administration.

Cisco Certified Network Associate (CCNA) – Intermediate networking certification for those pursuing careers as network engineers.

CompTIA Security+ – Entry-level cybersecurity certification for those transitioning into security analyst roles.

Microsoft Certified: Azure Fundamentals or AWS Certified Cloud Practitioner – Certifications for cloud computing careers.

Linux+ or LPIC-1 – Linux certifications for those moving into system administration.

Microsoft 365 Certified: Modern Desktop Administrator – Ideal for professionals working with Windows environments.

Certifications help IT professionals gain credibility, improve job prospects, and increase earning potential. Employers often prioritize candidates who have certifications relevant to their desired roles.

Gaining hands-on experience is just as important as obtaining certifications. Helpdesk analysts can expand their technical skills by taking on additional responsibilities, volunteering for IT projects, or building a home lab. Setting up virtual machines using VMware or

VirtualBox, configuring a test network with Cisco Packet Tracer, or experimenting with cloud services on AWS Free Tier or Azure Sandbox provides practical experience in specialized IT fields. Creating personal projects, such as automating tasks with PowerShell, setting up a Linux server, or practicing cybersecurity techniques in a controlled environment, helps build technical confidence and problem-solving abilities.

Networking within the IT industry also plays a key role in career advancement. Connecting with professionals in the desired field through LinkedIn, attending industry events, and joining online communities increases opportunities for mentorship and job referrals. Many IT professionals find new career opportunities through networking, referrals, and professional associations rather than traditional job applications. Engaging in technology forums, Reddit communities like r/sysadmin and r/cybersecurity, or Discord groups for IT professionals can provide insights and guidance from experienced individuals who have transitioned from helpdesk to other roles.

One of the best ways to gain real-world experience in a specialized field while working in helpdesk is to shadow senior IT staff and ask for hands-on training opportunities. Many system administrators, network engineers, and cybersecurity professionals are willing to mentor helpdesk analysts who show interest in learning. Offering to assist with server maintenance, help configure network equipment, or document security policies can provide valuable exposure to advanced IT tasks and technologies.

Improving soft skills is just as important as technical skills when transitioning to a higher-level IT role. Advanced IT positions require strong problem-solving, project management, and communication skills. System administrators and network engineers must collaborate with multiple teams, document system configurations, and explain technical concepts to non-technical users. Cybersecurity professionals often need to educate employees on security best practices, conduct risk assessments, and respond to incidents quickly and efficiently. Helpdesk analysts who demonstrate leadership, teamwork, and customer service excellence increase their chances of moving into management or specialized technical roles.

Once a helpdesk analyst has developed the necessary skills and experience, applying for internal promotions or external job opportunities is the next step. Many organizations prefer to promote from within, making internal job openings an excellent opportunity for career advancement. Helpdesk professionals should regularly check internal job postings, express interest in available roles, and discuss career goals with managers or HR representatives. If internal opportunities are limited, updating a resume, optimizing a LinkedIn profile, and applying for specialized IT positions externally can open doors to new career paths.

Customizing a resume and cover letter for specific roles is crucial when transitioning to a new IT position. A resume should highlight relevant technical skills, certifications, hands-on projects, and any experience beyond traditional helpdesk responsibilities. Including personal IT projects, such as configuring a home lab, managing a cloud-based server, or writing PowerShell scripts, demonstrates initiative and technical ability. Providing quantifiable achievements, such as 'resolved an average of 50+ support tickets per week while assisting the system administration team with Windows Server maintenance,' adds value to a resume.

Practicing for technical interviews is also essential. Many specialized IT roles require candidates to demonstrate their problem-solving skills, troubleshooting abilities, and knowledge of industry best practices. Reviewing common interview questions, setting up mock interviews, and taking online assessments help prepare for technical evaluations and real-world scenario discussions. Many cybersecurity roles include practical exercises or security challenges, while network and cloud-related roles may require candidates to explain system configurations or troubleshoot network issues live during an interview.

Helpdesk analysts who proactively learn new technologies, seek mentorship, gain certifications, and take on additional IT responsibilities can successfully transition to higher-paying and more specialized IT careers. By developing a clear career path, continuously improving technical skills, and building professional connections, helpdesk professionals can achieve long-term growth in the IT industry.

Leadership Skills and Moving into IT Management

Developing leadership skills is essential for IT professionals who aspire to move into IT management roles. Transitioning from a technical position to a leadership role requires more than just technical expertise—it demands strong communication, strategic thinking, problem-solving, and team management skills. IT managers oversee teams, projects, budgets, and technology implementations, making their role critical to an organization's success. Helpdesk analysts and IT support specialists who develop leadership qualities can position themselves for career growth in IT management by taking on additional responsibilities, learning business strategies, and refining their ability to lead and motivate teams.

One of the first steps toward IT leadership is demonstrating initiative in a current role. Leadership is not just about holding a management title—it is about taking ownership of projects, mentoring colleagues, and finding ways to improve IT operations. Helpdesk analysts can start by leading process improvements, documenting best practices, training new hires, or assisting with complex technical escalations. Volunteering to take on challenging assignments, proposing efficiency improvements, and assisting managers in decision-making processes showcases leadership potential and prepares individuals for higher-level responsibilities.

Effective communication skills are fundamental for IT managers. Unlike technical roles that focus primarily on troubleshooting and problem resolution, IT management requires the ability to translate complex technical information into business terms for executives and stakeholders. IT managers must also mediate conflicts, provide constructive feedback, and ensure clear communication between technical teams and non-technical departments. Developing strong verbal and written communication skills helps IT professionals deliver presentations, write detailed reports, and articulate IT strategies to leadership teams.

Understanding business and IT alignment is another critical aspect of moving into IT management. IT professionals must go beyond technical knowledge and develop an understanding of how IT supports business objectives, reduces operational costs, and enhances productivity. Learning about budgeting, IT service management (ITSM), key performance indicators (KPIs), and project management methodologies helps IT professionals make data-driven decisions that align with company goals. Gaining exposure to financial planning, IT procurement, and cost-benefit analysis allows future IT managers to make strategic decisions about software investments, hardware upgrades, and cloud migrations.

Time management and prioritization skills become increasingly important in IT leadership roles. IT managers must handle multiple projects, coordinate team efforts, and address critical system issues while meeting business deadlines. Learning to delegate tasks, manage workloads efficiently, and focus on high-impact projects ensures that IT teams remain productive and avoid burnout. Using project management tools such as Trello, Asana, or Microsoft Planner helps IT leaders organize tasks, set deadlines, and monitor team progress.

Developing team management skills is essential for transitioning into IT leadership. IT managers are responsible for hiring, training, mentoring, and evaluating employees. They must foster a positive team culture, resolve conflicts, and ensure that team members have the resources and support needed to succeed. Building a strong IT team requires recognizing individual strengths, providing opportunities for professional growth, and encouraging collaboration. Leading by example, maintaining transparency, and actively listening to team concerns help IT managers build trust and credibility.

Project management expertise is another key competency for IT leaders. Many IT managers oversee software deployments, system upgrades, cloud migrations, and security initiatives. Understanding Agile, Scrum, ITIL, and DevOps methodologies enables IT professionals to lead projects efficiently. Earning a Project Management Professional (PMP) certification, Certified Scrum Master (CSM), or ITIL certification enhances project management skills and demonstrates leadership capabilities.

Strategic decision-making is a crucial responsibility of IT managers. Leaders must analyze technical challenges, assess risks, and implement solutions that align with long-term business goals. Developing critical thinking and problem-solving skills ensures that IT professionals can make informed decisions in high-pressure situations, such as security incidents, system outages, or infrastructure failures. Understanding disaster recovery planning, risk management, and compliance requirements prepares IT professionals to handle crisis situations effectively.

Networking and building professional relationships help IT professionals transition into leadership roles. Attending IT conferences, leadership seminars, and industry networking events allows professionals to connect with experienced IT managers, CIOs, and business leaders who can provide mentorship and career guidance. Engaging with LinkedIn groups, technology forums, and IT leadership communities helps aspiring managers learn from industry experts and stay updated on best practices in IT governance, cybersecurity policies, and emerging technologies.

Continuous learning is essential for IT professionals aspiring to move into leadership roles. Technology evolves rapidly, and IT managers must stay informed about new developments, industry trends, and security threats. Pursuing advanced IT certifications, business management courses, or leadership training programs strengthens qualifications for senior IT positions. Many future IT managers enroll in Master of Business Administration (MBA) programs with an IT focus or obtain certifications such as Certified Information Systems Manager (CISM), Certified in the Governance of Enterprise IT (CGEIT), or Certified Technology Manager (CTM).

IT leadership also requires emotional intelligence (EQ) and adaptability. Effective leaders remain calm under pressure, handle workplace conflicts professionally, and motivate teams through difficult challenges. They understand the importance of empathy, active listening, and fostering a collaborative work environment. IT managers who build strong relationships with their teams enhance team morale, productivity, and job satisfaction.

Aspiring IT managers should seek mentorship and career development opportunities to accelerate their transition into leadership. Finding a mentor within the organization or industry provides valuable insights into management responsibilities, decision-making processes, and leadership challenges. Many organizations offer leadership development programs, management training courses, and cross-functional projects that help IT professionals gain the experience needed for senior roles.

Once an IT professional has developed leadership skills, business acumen, and project management experience, applying for IT management roles becomes the next step. Updating a resume to highlight leadership achievements, strategic decision-making, and project successes strengthens applications for IT supervisor, team lead, and IT manager positions. Practicing for behavioral and technical interviews, preparing answers for leadership-focused questions, and demonstrating problem-solving abilities increases the likelihood of securing a management position.

Transitioning into IT management requires a combination of technical expertise, leadership development, business knowledge, and strategic planning. By taking initiative, improving communication skills, learning about IT governance, and gaining experience in team management, IT professionals can successfully move into leadership roles and contribute to the long-term success of their organizations.

Final Thoughts: Mastering the Helpdesk Analyst Role

Becoming a highly skilled helpdesk analyst requires more than just technical expertise. While troubleshooting hardware and software issues is a core responsibility, the role demands a combination of problem-solving abilities, communication skills, patience, adaptability, and continuous learning. A helpdesk analyst is often the first point of contact for users experiencing technical difficulties, making them an essential part of an organization's IT support structure. Mastering this role involves not only excelling at resolving technical issues but also providing exceptional customer service and understanding how IT contributes to business operations.

One of the most critical skills a helpdesk analyst must develop is effective troubleshooting. Every technical issue presents a unique challenge, and analysts must learn to diagnose problems methodically. Following a structured approach, such as the Identify, Analyze, Test, Implement, and Verify method, ensures that issues are resolved efficiently without unnecessary guesswork. Analysts must also familiarize themselves with common troubleshooting tools such as event logs, network diagnostic utilities, remote desktop applications, and system monitoring tools to diagnose and resolve issues effectively.

Communication plays a crucial role in providing IT support. Many end-users are not technically proficient, and it is the analyst's job to translate complex IT concepts into simple, easy-to-understand explanations. A skilled helpdesk analyst knows how to ask the right questions, actively listen, and provide clear instructions. Written communication is equally important, as analysts often need to document tickets, create knowledge base articles, and respond to users via email or chat. Well-documented ticket notes and troubleshooting steps help ensure that issues can be followed up efficiently and that escalation teams have the necessary context to take over if required.

Patience and empathy are key attributes of a successful helpdesk analyst. Users may be frustrated, stressed, or under pressure to meet deadlines when they encounter technical issues. Maintaining a calm and professional demeanor, even in challenging situations, helps to de-escalate conflicts and reassure users that their concerns are being addressed. A great helpdesk analyst does not just fix technical problems—they also ensure that users feel supported throughout the troubleshooting process.

Time management and prioritization are crucial skills in a helpdesk environment. Analysts often handle multiple tickets, phone calls, and urgent requests simultaneously. Knowing how to prioritize critical issues, manage response times, and balance workload efficiently prevents unnecessary delays and improves overall service quality. Many organizations use Service Level Agreements (SLAs) to define response and resolution times, making it essential for analysts to track their progress and meet these expectations consistently.

Staying up to date with technology trends, security best practices, and industry developments is necessary for continued success in a helpdesk role. IT is a fast-evolving field, and new software, security threats, and troubleshooting methodologies emerge regularly. Helpdesk analysts should make use of online courses, certification programs, technology blogs, and IT forums to expand their knowledge and stay ahead of industry changes. Certifications such as CompTIA A+, ITIL, Microsoft 365 Certified, and Google IT Support Professional not only enhance technical expertise but also improve career prospects.

Mastering remote support tools is increasingly important as more organizations adopt hybrid and remote work environments. Helpdesk analysts must be proficient in using remote desktop applications, virtual private networks (VPNs), cloud-based ticketing systems, and collaboration tools. Supporting users in various locations requires adaptability and strong diagnostic skills, as analysts cannot always rely on direct physical access to devices.

Understanding IT security principles is another key aspect of the helpdesk role. Analysts must educate users on safe computing practices, password security, multi-factor authentication (MFA), and phishing awareness. Many security breaches occur due to human error, and helpdesk teams play a vital role in minimizing risks by reinforcing security policies and identifying potential threats early. Analysts should be familiar with common cyber threats, endpoint security tools, and access control mechanisms to help protect both users and company data.

Documentation and knowledge sharing contribute significantly to long-term efficiency in IT support. Creating detailed troubleshooting guides, frequently asked questions (FAQs), and step-by-step instructions allows users to solve common issues independently and reduces the overall ticket volume. A well-maintained knowledge base benefits both end-users and IT teams by ensuring that solutions are standardized, repeatable, and accessible.

Collaboration with other IT teams is essential for handling complex technical issues, escalating unresolved tickets, and contributing to IT projects. Helpdesk analysts frequently work with network engineers, system administrators, security teams, and software developers to troubleshoot and resolve infrastructure, software, or access-related problems. Building strong professional relationships within the IT department ensures efficient communication, faster issue resolution, and opportunities for learning and career growth.

Professionalism and accountability are key traits of a great helpdesk analyst. IT support is a high-responsibility role, as end-users rely on the helpdesk to keep their work running smoothly. Analysts must take ownership of the tickets they handle, follow up on unresolved issues, and ensure that users receive timely updates. Maintaining a positive attitude, delivering high-quality support, and striving for continuous improvement makes a significant difference in the overall user experience.

For those looking to advance their careers, leveraging the helpdesk role as a stepping stone is a smart strategy. Many IT professionals start in helpdesk positions before moving into networking, system administration, cybersecurity, cloud computing, software engineering, or IT management. By gaining experience, earning certifications, taking on additional responsibilities, and developing leadership skills, helpdesk analysts can transition into more advanced roles within IT.

Mentorship and professional networking can also accelerate career growth. Connecting with experienced IT professionals, joining LinkedIn groups, participating in industry discussions, and attending tech conferences provides valuable insights and career opportunities. Many organizations also offer internal promotions and training programs, making it beneficial for analysts to express interest in career development and new challenges.

The helpdesk analyst role is an essential part of IT operations, ensuring that employees and businesses can function efficiently. Mastering this role involves technical excellence, strong communication, time management, security awareness, and a proactive mindset. Helpdesk analysts who continually learn, adapt, and take initiative will not only excel in their current roles but also open doors to new career opportunities and long-term success in the IT industry.